DON
WILLIAMS

D0849326

CHILDREN OF THE EVENING

CHILDREN OF THE EVENING

TRUDEE ABLE-PETERSON

G. P. Putnam's Sons
New York

Copyright © 1981 by Trudee Able-Peterson
All rights reserved. This book, or parts thereof,
may not be reproduced in any form without permission.
Published simultaneously in Canada
by Academic Press Canada Limited, Toronto.

LIBRARY OF CONGRESS CATALOGING IN PUBLICATION DATA
Able-Peterson, Trudee.
    Children of the evening.

    1. Prostitution, Juvenile—New York (N.Y.)
2. Runaway children—New York (N.Y.) 3. Social
work with prostitutes—New York (N.Y.) I. Title.
HQ146.N7A34   1981   363.4'4'088055   81-12183
ISBN 0-399-12631-7   AACR2

PRINTED IN THE UNITED STATES OF AMERICA

Acknowledgments

I would like to thank my husband and children, without whose support and encouragement I couldn't have made it through the often painful writing of this book.

I would also like to thank the book's godmother, Nancy Nicholas. It was she who first believed I could write this book.

If it had not been for Jane Krahn, Mary Krahn, and June Fleeson Srouefe, I might still be working in a Chinese restaurant. I am forever indebted to them for their participation in my life.

George Trapp and Warren McGyness are two of the cops out there trying to protect and save these children—our children—from death and destruction. All of us should thank them and others like them.

My editor, Faith Sale, has believed in this book from the beginning. I thank her in the name of the children who so badly need this story to be told.

Finally, thanks, Kathy Gleason, for your initial help with my proposal and your supportive and artistic encouragement.

Marge L. Mikkelson, thanks for being my lifelong friend through all things.

This book is based upon the author's actual experiences, but names have been changed and composites created to protect the true identities of the people involved; any resemblance to persons living or dead is purely coincidental.

To the memory of H.P.
Child, you have not died in vain.

CHILDREN OF THE EVENING

THE CENTER was packed last night. With a little luck, there'd be some discharges on today's shift. Walking up the stairs on my way in, I'd heard the voices of the kids calling to me. "Ms. Peterson, I need medicine." "Ms. Peterson, can I take a shower?" "Ms. Peterson, when are you gonna talk to me?" "Ms. Peterson, somebody stole my socks." Like baby birds peeping loudly for their sustenance. Filling them up seemed an awesome task.

They came to the Center in search of food, shelter, medical care, clothing. But, most of all, they were in search of caring. Sometimes, when I came home, I would lie awake thinking about the children, about the pain and desperation, the confusion in their young eyes. It stayed with me.

So I was glad to be on the late shift today. I never could have gotten up for the early one.

11

The phone rang, jolting me from my reflections.

It was Jack, an administrator at the Center. "Have you seen the newspapers today, Trudee?" he asked me.

"No. Why?"

"There's a picture in the *Post* of a girl. She was found murdered last night. She looks familiar to a couple of the staff."

"Who is it, Jack?" I wanted to slam the phone down before he could answer.

"I don't know. The paper says Sharon Styles."

The horror stories my young prostitutes told me flashed in my head. This trick did this, this one that, so-and-so puts a knife to a girl's throat before she blew him.

"I don't know her." I let out the breath I didn't realize I was holding. Thank God it wasn't Delia. Or Melissa. Melissa, age thirteen, missing from the Center for three weeks. Or even me.

This *could* have happened to me in the days when I'd gone into dark rooms with strange men for money. I shuddered remembering how close I'd been to death a few times eight long years ago, even though I'd lived a more exclusive call-girl existence. I knew many prostitutes were murdered every year, and many of the cases went unsolved. Maybe no one cared about them. Maybe, because they lived between the cracks of society, their murderers were often impossible to trace.

I knew these young street girls had it much worse than I'd had it. Getting into strange cars, driving away to rented rooms with men they knew nothing about.

"Maybe you'd better pick up a paper on the way to work," Jack insisted.

Work was counseling sexually exploited children in New York City's Times Square. Trying to get them off the streets and out of the clutches of pimps. Away from the self-destructive behavior, the low self-image, that convinced them they were only worth a fifteen-dollar car trick. I was trying to build a relationship of trust so that if they wanted off the streets and out of "the life," they'd come to me for help. Then I could try to help sort out their sordid lives. And didn't I know that story best? Not from learned social-work theories, but from my own painful memories.

My stomach did a small flip at the insistence in Jack's voice. He wasn't telling me everything. "Okay, Jack, what else?"

"We just want you to see a paper, Trudee."

She wasn't anybody I knew, this Sharon Styles. I kept repeating that as I dressed and searched for my keys. Whoever she was I felt awful about her, but she *wasn't* one of my girls.

I bought the *Post* at the stand a few blocks away and walked back toward my apartment, turning the pages slowly. On page four was Heather Paulson's pretty face, her passive eyes staring out at me. I stopped walking and gazed horrified at the picture of the seventeen-year-old girl I'd worked with just months ago. I felt sick and stopped to lean against a building.

The facts I had on Heather immediately flashed through my mind. Place of birth: California. In foster care at age five; numerous unsuccessful foster homes for the next eight years. Age first run: thirteen. Age entered prostitution: thirteen. In and out of detention and foster care for a few years, then vanished from the systems that never met her needs, for good. To the streets of California, Las Vegas, and finally New York City she went, searching for some love or meaning in her life.

Heather, oh God, not Heather. So passive, so vic-

13

timized by an unfair beginning. Heather, such a sweet, lonely, withdrawn girl.

I snapped the paper shut, trying to block the details. Walking through the cold March wind, I shivered. Heather's body found nude in a parking lot, without her *legs!* I cried unashamedly as I walked along.

In my apartment I set the newspaper down and sat on the other side of the room, staring at it. What happened to her legs? Hot sweat crawled on my skin. I started for the bathroom and made the sink, gagging. I washed my face in the tub then cleaned the sink.

Sick, oh sickness, crazy motherfucker cut her legs off. Was she alive when he did it? Violent, brutal, sick. I rubbed my thighs.

I skimmed the article again and stopped at the part about her legs, unable to read any more. I knew they had no suspects. They probably never will, I thought. A crazy, faceless trick. I wondered if he'd gotten off on it.

I had to stop thinking like this. I had to talk to someone.

I dialed work slowly; the ringing sounded far away.

"Jack Innes, please," I said. And when he picked up his phone I blurted out, "Jack, it's Heather Paulson," and started to cry again.

"You knew her." A statement, not a question.

"Jack, do you remember her?"

"I don't think so, but I'm not with the kids as much as you. I'm really sorry, Trudee. Are you all right?"

"I'll be down shortly."

"Are you sure—"

"I said I'll be down, Jack." I had to get out of the house, be with other people, be at work, take a head count on my other girls.

"Okay, Trudee, I think you better call the police and

identify her. Stop in my office when you get here, okay?"

"Goodbye, Jack."

I hung up and dialed the number for the Youth Morals Squad, the special police unit that worked with this population of kids.

As I waited for Sergeant Barnes to come to the phone, I realized how much I liked and trusted this man, a cop! Strange, when I'd been in "the life" myself I'd hated cops—always afraid of a bust. I remembered the cop who flashed a badge on me in Atlanta. He wanted free sex.

But I had realized his badge was from another county and told him to stick it in his ear.

I knew that Sergeant Barnes wouldn't frighten or take advantage of a prostitute. The street girls and boys were his kids too. I'd developed a keen sense of instinct after all that intimacy. It had kept me out of jail and away from the crazies. Why hadn't Heather learned the same? Or hadn't she cared? A death wish?

"Trudee?" came the voice of my cop friend.

"Frank, Sharon Styles, she's Heather Paulson, I worked with her some months ago."

"I figured that wasn't her real name. Where's she from?"

"California. Frank?"

"Yeah?"

"Who did it? Who cut off that girl's legs and slit her throat?"

"We don't know, Trudee," he answered softly. "There's plenty of sick ones out there. They haven't found her legs."

"I know, Frank. Oh God, I don't feel so hot."

For a few seconds the line was silent.

"Frank, this had to be a sick, crazy trick. It doesn't

15

sound like a pimp's style, does it?"

"No, I think it was a trick, definitely."

We both knew that pimps use mental cruelty and beatings to teach their girls a lesson, but when they kill, it's more often by accident.

"Sex and murder always make me think of tricks, Frank, not pimps."

"This guy's really weird."

I realized that we were both assuming it was a man. It was impossible, somehow, to imagine otherwise. "Do you have *any* idea, any leads?"

"Nah, nothing, not at this point."

"Frank, find him, please!"

"Call me if you want. I'll be here."

"Thanks."

After hanging up with Frank Barnes, I climbed into the shower with *Psycho*-like thoughts swirling in my head. I thought of movies like *Klute* and *Frenzy*. Heather had actually lived out one of these horrible, violent plots. Heather's life would match any Hitchcock creation.

I reached for a towel and dried myself automatically, my body functioning while my brain, numb and shocked, ached to have another chance to deal with Heather's life.

I remembered my logs. The first months I'd worked at the Center I kept notes regarding cases that were problematic for me, so I could talk them out in my

16

supervision with Jack. I found the log on Heather. I also found three receipts from Bellevue I'd forgotten to put in her file at work. My eyes clung to her name stamped in clinic blue. I sat in the doorway of the closet leaning against the doorframe and read the log. My first fatality in three years' work with these kids. I guess I should be grateful, I thought bitterly.

My mind reached back to the year before, to a time when Heather and I were sitting alone in the Center's dining room.

"Heather," I had said, "you can't just float from guy to guy on the street, selling yourself for a bottle and a place to lay your head. You're hurting yourself so much."

"I know," she said, tears welling up in her blue eyes. She shrugged her shoulders. Her eyes were older than sixteen summers. I looked into her pretty soft face framed with brilliant red hair. She looked so tired and spent. I recalled that she was recovering from hepatitis then.

"Maybe you could work independently in California or Las Vegas, but these New York pimps will grab you in a minute."

"There's nothing to go back to, anywhere," she said dejectedly, almost apologizing. "I'm sorry I'm in your way."

How many times had I heard that sound in the voices of these young people? "What happened to your family?" I asked gently.

"I don't know," she sighed. "I've been in foster homes since I was five."

"Were they pretty bad?"

"Oh, some bad, some okay, but mostly nothing . . . I don't know."

17

She was very withdrawn. I wasn't sure if she had given up trying to express her feelings or if she had never learned how.

"When did you leave the last foster home, Heather?"

"I was about fifteen, fourteen and a half . . . I kept running away at thirteen, fourteen. They'd take me to another home when they caught me."

"And when did you get into prostitution?"

"When I first started running. I did it to eat and buy clothes. First, just to eat," her soft voice explained. She had such a gentle demeanor, she didn't seem hard or tough at all. I told her this. She smiled, just a small curve of her weary mouth.

It was getting noisy in the dining room area. I knew we would have no peace as soon as the kids drifted in for dinner.

"C'mon, honey, let's see if we can find a quiet spot, okay?"

She stood immediately, as if she had military orders, and followed me willingly. My God, I thought, she'd be a piece of cake for anybody who came on half-kind to her.

I put my arm around her shoulders as we left the dining room.

"You know, my mother had red hair and freckles, I'm awfully partial to them," I confided to her. She accepted my arm, seeming glad to be leaning on someone. She gave me another little half smile, her eyes a little warmer, not so lifeless.

We found some space alone to continue our talk, but I knew we wouldn't have it long, as dinnertime brought all the kids back to the Center.

"Have you been drinking for a long time, Heather?" I had noticed how badly she shook.

"Yes. . . . It takes away the pain . . . for a while."

"Would you consider a de-tox program or a hospital?" I urged.

She gazed ahead as though she hadn't heard me. I wondered if other people had sung her the same tune.

"Heather?"

"Where?"

"I don't know. I'll check into it tomorrow, okay? Think you can make it through the night?"

She nodded. "I'm pretty tired and I have really bad pains in my stomach."

She was very pale. "Would you like me to get someone to take you to a hospital?" As an assistant supervisor, I myself couldn't leave the Center.

"No, I'd like to lie down for a while though."

"How about food, honey?"

"I'm not hungry, just tired."

"Okay, let me find you some space, and if you feel any worse let me know."

She fell asleep in the corner on two large chair pillows. I checked her occasionally but she was out cold.

I gave the casework information to my supervisor at the 9 P.M. update. "Rick, she's a very sweet kid, but really messed up from everything. She's been alone for two and a half, three years. Into prostitution, booze, pills. She really needs de-tox and medical care, but most of all, someone to care for her. Where can I refer her?"

He shook his head. I knew the answer before he spoke. I'd been a counselor in New York City for two months and I knew the systems. I had just been promoted to assistant supervisor. Services in New York for a girl like Heather were extremely limited. There were none designed specially for prostitutes, except our Center, and we weren't set up for long-term help,

19

just for crisis intervention. It wasn't enough.

"A drug program is the only place, Trudee, you know that," Rick said kindly. He knew how I felt about these girls.

"But Rick, she needs so much more than that. I don't think she'd stay at one very long."

"I know." Rick sighed, putting a big comforting hand on my shoulder. I appreciated the silence that followed. At least Rick didn't tell me not to get "overinvolved," as did most of the supervisors. If these kids—if Heather—had someone *involved*, let alone overinvolved, in their lives, they wouldn't be here now.

I woke up Heather before bedtime to see if she'd eat something. I pushed her damp sleep-wet hair off her cheek. Did she feel warm? "Heather, Heather, wake up, honey."

She moaned in pain as she came to.

"Heather, I think you should go to the hospital."

"Okay. It hurts pretty bad."

I took her temperature, just a little above normal— good. I arranged for a staff escort.

"I'll see you tomorrow, okay?" I reassured her as I helped her into a cab in front of the Center. Her eyes clung to me. "I wish I could go with you, honey, but I can't," I said lamely. "I'll call later to see how you are."

The hospital didn't keep Heather that night. They gave her a few mild tranquilizers and an appointment

20

for a few days hence. I was glad to see her the next day when I walked into the Center.

"Hi, how ya doin' today?"

"Okay." Her smile made me feel good inside. And she looked better today.

"What happened at the hospital last night?"

"They just made an appointment for the clinic on Tuesday. I feel better though."

Her complexion wasn't so pale. Maybe the rest and food were working.

"Having any pains, hon?"

"Not as bad." She still shook.

"Good." I felt her forehead. She was cool. I could tell she enjoyed my small attentions.

"Let me check in upstairs and I'll talk to you in a little while."

"Okay."

Rick, the supervisor that evening, told me that one of the drug programs had accepted Heather, and that she would leave tomorrow.

"Oh, so soon," I said.

"I know. Crisis intervention, it gets on my nerves too. You're just getting somewhere with a kid and they're gone the next day. It's really a burn-out for staff. Heather needs the medical care and drying-out time they can give her though, Trudee."

"What about the caring, Rick, will they give her that? Will they make her feel that she's worthwhile? Will they keep her off the streets?"

"Trudee," Rick began tiredly.

"I'm sorry, Rick, I know you can't do anything about it. It's not your fault." I sighed, feeling extremely helpless. "I'll prep her today, I'm pretty sure she'll go. Rick, she's so soft, in spite of the street years, she's still

21

so vulnerable. It scares me—it's like she's willing to let life do anything to her. She has no fight-back power. She'd never hurt a fly, but she's destroying herself. A willing sacrifice."

"Maybe you can keep in touch with the drug program and see how she's doing," he offered.

"You can bet on it. Okay, what's the house look like today?"

"Ten discharges yesterday, but eight intakes on the overnight brings the census back up to sixty-eight. I listed casework for you to hand out to staff. You take the top priority kids. I'll work the dinner hour downstairs, you take it up here. Take a look at staffing and see who hasn't done maintenance lately."

"Thanks."

"If you're gonna be a supervisor soon you have to learn to delegate responsibility."

"Yeah, yeah, delegate and de-escalate, the supervisor's key to a good house." I smiled at Rick. He was determined that I become the first full-time female supervisor, and I was beginning to believe he'd get me there.

"Rick, I'd like to spend some extra time with Heather. Don't worry, I'll get everything else done."

"I'm not worried, your work has been excellent, and if you can work it out, it's fine with me."

Everywhere I turned the first few hours, Heather seemed to be near me. I gave her arm a reassuring squeeze now and again. It was very busy, and the needs of these kids were boundless.

As I went toward the corner pillow Heather had finally settled on, a young girl had an epileptic seizure in my path.

"Somebody get me a spoon, quick," I ordered as I knelt beside her. A few kids went scurrying for the spoon and to call Rick, as others gaped frightened, mesmerized at something they weren't familiar with. I was grateful when Rick took over with a nurse from the volunteer staff. I had never been very good with medical situations.

I finally plopped down beside Heather in a relatively quiet corner. I noticed she didn't mingle too much with the other kids. She still looked pale and shaky.

"Need a drink, babe?"

"Yeah," she answered.

"I know," I took one of her hands in mine and took a deep breath.

"I once lived the same life, Heather. Prostitution, drugs, pillar to post."

"You did?" Her eyes showed surprise and interest.

"What's really important is that I made it out. It wasn't easy, and I won't pretend it was. It took a great deal of strength and caring about myself. You have to believe you're worth something. You *are*, Heather. You've got to believe that to begin with. You're a very nice person, Heather, you are!" I looked into a pair of disbelieving blue eyes. "Please try to make it out, it's so dangerous in this city, babe, it's not like any other city."

She stared at the floor. "You know you're pretty on the outside, attractive, but that's not what I mean. You're nice inside, gentle and soft."

I could see she wasn't going to buy this, but I had to try, and it was the truth. "Those are beautiful qualities, but not for the streets, honey. You're too fragile for the street."

Her sad face just sort of hung there in the air, as if it was ready to be kicked or something. She looked like she could use about a hundred years' worth of sleep.

"Heather, I felt the same way once. Like I was worth

nothing, like I didn't deserve anything better than shit. It wasn't true, Heather! I'm a human being, I have as much right as anybody to happiness. So do you. Happiness and decency and comfort and love. And nobody better ever tell me I don't deserve them."

Her head dropped to one side and she sighed deeply. I wanted alternately to shake life into her and to take her in my arms and rock her to sleep. I wished I had a magic spell that would propel her back to age five, to start all over again on a loving path. Self-destruction is learned behavior, unnatural behavior. Someone had to have taught her to hate herself. All the young prostitutes I'd worked with were similar to Heather. Some were aggressive, self-destructive and others, like Heather, were passive. But, no matter how it came down, they had all learned they were worthless.

"Honey, if only you could begin to care about yourself, just a little. See, I had to stand up and say, 'Damn it, Trudee is worth something. She's better than just laying under some damn trick and gettin' high to do it. She's a whole lot better.' That's what I had to begin saying. Nothing changed until I could do that. And Heather, *I* can care about you, but unless *you* do, it's no good."

She sighed again as though it were an impossible task.

"I don't know what to do any more, where to start," she said wearily.

"You've got to start fighting, Heather, fight back! Don't let life just sweep you up and deposit you anywhere it wants to. Fight it! Right now you can begin with your health and the booze. Look, we have a drug program that will accept you tomorrow. Will you go? Will you try, Heather?"

24

"I have no choice. I don't know anybody in New York. I'm tired of waking up in the gutters, tired of turning tricks. I hate it! Tired of having guys I pick up throw me out the next morning."

I had the sensation she was bleeding, gushing her life out on the pillow.

"It isn't good enough to just go there, Heather," I said shaking my head. "You've got to try to make it or it just won't work. Please try, honey, you're still so young. I didn't start over till I was twenty-nine. Think about it."

She gathered hope from the fire in my eyes and said, "Okay, I'll really try it." There was more life and conviction in her voice than I'd heard so far.

"Good for you, girl!" I cheered, sincerely feeling like I'd touched something in her. "Listen, if you don't like it, come back and I'll try to find you something else. Let me be your anchor, Heather. If things go really badly, come back to me."

"Thank you," she said softly. I kissed her cheek. On the big orange pillows a few feet away, a young girl jumped in her sleep. Heather and I both started, surprised by this movement, then we both laughed a little, feeling some relief from the intensity of our session.

"I'll talk to you at bedtime, honey," I said as I stood up to leave her.

I didn't want her to go, I wanted to keep her, to really work with her on a long-term basis. Maybe then her self-esteem would begin to change. I knew I was sending her into a program I didn't have much faith in. I didn't trust anybody with these girls except myself. I kneeled down beside her once again.

"Heather, I'll call soon to see how you're doing. If you can't hack it, please come back—I mean that.

Sometimes, when life starts us out with a kick, we feel it's what we deserve and we continue to kick ourselves. You don't deserve kicking. You're really a nice person—I like you a lot."

She still hadn't bought it, but she gave me another one of her rare half smiles. She really looked tired. Heather would need to be told these things over and over, to be shown them, to feel caring and concern. It would take a lot of consciousness-raising to change Heather's image of herself.

I turned and walked across the floor. "Hi, Ms. Peterson," several of the kids called.

"Hi, Loretta. How ya doin', Doug, did you get your birth certificate today? Good. Perry, watch the cutting up, someone may get hurt, then angry."

"Trudee, Rick says you should eat now before we start the kids, or you won't have a chance," one of the male staff said.

"Okay, thanks."

When I sat down at the wooden table in the small dining room I suddenly felt sick. My head ached and my stomach lurched as I looked down at the food. I couldn't eat.

I motioned to Rick who was nearby, bending over a very young girl on the couch. By the time he came over, my head was pounding.

"What's up, food that bad?" Rick asked, noticing my untouched tray.

"Rick, all of a sudden I feel terribly ill. I don't know what came over me, I felt fine when I came in today."

"Maybe you're catching something from one of the kids, Trudee."

"I don't know. It came on so suddenly."

"Wait a minute, what were you doing before you felt sick?"

"I was downstairs talking to Heather. That's probably it. We had a very intense session. She's so sick, I can feel it in her, physically and emotionally. Can it really transfer like this? Jesus!"

"I've seen a lot stranger things than this. Why not take two aspirins, then throw yourself into something physical, work it out of your system, it might really help."

"I sure need to try something," I said weakly.

"If it doesn't help in a half hour I'll send you home. It could be flu or something."

I went to the clothing room and sorted clothing, swept and lugged the heavy bags of clothing I'd sorted out to the outside room for a pickup by the Salvation Army the next day. I worked hard concentrating on the usual disarray and nothing else.

"Trudee, you all right?" I looked up to see Rick's worried face coming toward me.

"I think so. I just threw myself into taking care of this room."

"I guess you did, it looks better than it has in weeks."

"Thanks! It does have a little order now. I'm sure I can stay, I really feel better."

"Trudee, it's dangerous, what happened to you. You've got to watch yourself," Rick said. "I think you better bring it up the next time you have your supervision meeting with Jack. It warrants more discussion than we have time for right now."

"I will, Rick. I'm learning things slowly but surely. I know I have to learn to give good caring without losing myself. I admit it, I overidentify with this kind of kid. It's like seeing myself all over again."

"But if you don't watch it, you'll burn out. I've seen it happen."

"Thanks. Let's get out of here. I promise I'll bring it up with Jack next week."

Back on the second floor dinner was almost over. I hadn't realized almost two hours had passed. I was grateful to Rick for giving me the time to ease out. There was plenty I could have done upstairs, helping to control nearly seventy pushing, shoving, hungry kids, trying to keep fights from breaking out.

At the end of the night I was completely exhausted from emotional strain as well as physical work. I had taken care of all the top priority cases, which involved researching family contacts for the Center's younger residents. I filled out contact sheets for them and attached them to their respective files. When I came to Heather's file, I was faced with a blank sheet of paper.

I thought about the drug programs. They offered a confrontational therapy approach. It was called breaking down the negative self-image. For drug addicts this seemed to be necessary. Certainly prostitutes use a lot of street drugs. But which came first? Usually the kids I worked with had begun taking drugs to escape the ugly, monotonous reality of prostitution.

Certainly Heather was dependent on alchohol and would get treatment for it in a place like this, but who would deal with the pain in her head regarding the countless men and the hundreds of times she'd given her young body to them?

There wasn't a specialized facility for kids like her, I knew that. I wanted so badly to work with her. I thought a supportive, loving approach might be better for the issues that led these kids to their present lifestyle.

I looked at the empty paper with Heather's name across the top. Society's undesirable, I thought. It didn't fit the quiet and gentle kid I'd met. A young girl trying not to take up too much space in a world that had never seemed to want her. I wrote on the sheet that Heather was emotionally unstable, physically ill, and dependent on alcohol. We had arranged a referral to a drug program for her, a "therapeutic community" as they were called.

I handed in my casework, helped the girls set up mats, and assigned bed space for the night. I hugged or kissed most of the girls goodnight. I believed in touch therapy, and unless the kids really made it clear they wouldn't, couldn't be touched, I used it. Usually they were starving for contact.

"I'm proud of you, kid, you made it through another night without a drink, and you're okay," I whispered to Heather as I bent down to pull the cover up over her shoulders. "How do you feel?"

"Not bad," she lied. I saw pain in her eyes. I kissed her goodnight. "I'll see you tomorrow. Sleep tight."

"Good night, Trudee, thanks."

It was the first time she'd used my name. For what, Heather, thanks for what? For sending you away?

Before I left for the night I made my nightly check on the girls' room and found them all sleeping soundly. Their faces in sleep looked so innocent and unsophisticated. I resented the changes that daylight would reveal in those faces: the bitterness, the pain, the hopelessness that girls like Heather felt.

I stepped carefully between the bed mats on the floor and tiptoed over to Heather's side. The little girl next to her was sucking her thumb. Heather's red hair was spread on the pillow framing her pretty face. She looked so peaceful. I bent down and kissed her cheek and she moved slightly, making a soft sleep sound.

"Good night, sweetheart," I whispered.

Goddamn it, she shouldn't be leaving here so soon! I should have more time with her! If I just had some time. What the hell can you do for someone in three days? I hated crisis intervention. I knew it was necessary but wished to hell I wasn't in it. I wanted to work long term with these girls. But nobody was doing it. Crisis intervention was the only service available to them. It wasn't enough.

I brushed Heather's hair, thinking, "I'll lose you, child, I'm afraid I'll lose you." I tried to will some strength into her, some motivation for her to care about herself.

The next afternoon I hugged Heather. For the last time, it turned out. She seemed frightened to leave me and clung to me for a brief few seconds. All of a sudden I felt sorry I had gotten close to her; it wasn't fair to open her up to caring and then send her away like this. It left her open, vulnerable. The unfairness of it choked me as I walked her down the stairs to the doorway.

"Please come back if you need me. Please, honey."

She nodded her head slightly but said nothing. I looked into her blue eyes once more. I could see she felt rejected, and it killed me.

And then she was gone.

"Goodbye, Heather," I repeated as they walked down the street. I stood in the bright daylight sunshine on the dirty street in front of the Center watching her and her escort move away down the sidewalk, into the busy crowd. My last sight of her was her beautiful red hair, swaying, between the heads of the other pedestrians.

I called the drug program every week or ten days. "She's doing fine," they assured me. I wanted to believe it.

Six weeks later I ran into one of the drug counselors. "How's Heather Paulson doing?"

"She left a week or so ago, Trudee."

"Oh, no."

"Yes, I really felt bad. She was doing well for the first month, then she just took off. One of the kids saw her on the street. She's hustling, I think." He shook his head.

From that day, I always looked for Heather in the Times Square streets. I never forgot her or any of the girls who floated out of my life.

I never saw her, but I would turn every time I saw a redhead. She never came back to see me. She had bought the street-life concept. Her feelings of low self-worth had devoured her like the streets of the teeming city. I figured she'd end up a shopping-bag lady someday, after the streets used up her youth and beauty. If she could stay alive out there.

Well, she hadn't. I still couldn't believe it. But finally I had pulled myself out of my memories and started to get dressed. I packed the ugly newspaper in my briefcase and quietly closed the door to my little apartment behind me.

I'd lived in New York six years, and I loved it, but I had never gotten used to the dirty subways. Today more than ever I hated them. I stared out the train windows, watching the uptown stations flash by. The air was thick and dense with bodies and odors, and I closed my eyes to at least shut out the sights, if not smells, counting the stops down to Times Square.

I climbed up through the grimy tunnels coated with spit and urine, up the gray-black litter-strewn stairs into the filth of Times Square. Forty-second Street, The Deuce, Forty-DuWop, the street kids called it. On one corner a disheveled and dirty young man lay sleeping soundly as the bustling crowds walked around him. If anyone wondered if he was really sleeping or perhaps dead, nobody stopped to find out.

I walked up the street toward the Center. The peep-show hawkers called their wares. "Beeyooteefull girls, live acts on stage!" Little Melissa had made her way into one of these shows. It wasn't unusual for thirteen- and fourteen-year-olds to work in these sex shops. Sly and sheepish, businessmen sneaked in and out of the doorways. "Only twenty-five cents, see the most beeyooteefull girls in the world!"

I wound through the crowd and down the street to the Center. I can't look for Heather any more, I thought, she'll never be on these ugly streets again.

I went straight to Jack's office. "I thought I'd be in early, instead I guess I'm late. Sorry. I found my old logs. Remember when I was in training, and you had me write those logs? I got wrapped up reading my feelings on the days I worked with Heather."

"I think I remember. Sit down, Trudee, I'll call your department and tell them you'll be a little late. I'd like to talk to you."

As Jack telephoned, I sank into the familiar black-and-chrome office chair where I'd learned so much in the last year. I was glad I was there. I knew Jack could help me deal with my feelings if anybody could.

He hung up. "Kelly offered to work a double shift if you don't feel you can work tonight," Jack said.

"No, I want to be busy tonight, I need to see the other girls, too."

"How are you feeling now, Trudee?"

"A little better. I needed to get out of the house. But I

feel guilty, Jack, I never helped her."

"Trudee, you mustn't personalize her death. You did what you could for her."

"Bullshit, Jack, she's dead. What did anybody do for her?"

"Heather had some free choices and a right to make them. Even danger leading to death is a choice."

"She never had a choice! Her life was all arranged, a big fucking mess she inherited!" I jumped up from the chair. "We've got to have a long-term shelter for these girls. Jack, she would have stayed with me, I know she would have!"

"It's not your fault, Trudee. We aren't a long-term facility."

"Yes, it is, the fault is mine and yours and everyone's! We can't pretend to treat these girls by putting Band-Aids on big gaping wounds. That's what I wrote in the log, Jack!"

"Look, we don't have the funds for a long-term facility. You have to think of all the good we do and the hundreds, thousands of kids who come to Times Square that we do help. You've helped a lot of those kids."

I knew, of course, that what Jack was saying was true. "Oh, I'm sorry. I guess it's going to take time to work this thing out. I'm never going to forget her, Jack. I'll work so much harder on the others!"

He came out from behind his desk and put an arm around my shoulder. The silence and the physical contact lent me strength and renewed my spirits.

*　　*　　*

As I walked through the Center heading for a staff meeting, my fellow workers, especially Jimmy, made a point of expressing their concern. They all knew about Heather. In the makeshift board room, I read through the review of the kids in-house and their plans. I felt relieved; it was good to have to think about those who were still alive and how to help them stay that way.

There were seventy-eight kids in-house. That night we would probably successfully place and discharge three or four and take in about eight, so it would be busy enough that I couldn't dwell on Heather's death.

The two women who ran the office had lists of staff and casework made up for me after the meeting.

"Thanks a lot. I really appreciate your help," I said as they left for the day. I did. Working with good, caring people made the work possible. As long as we all truly cared about the kids, we worked better and harder together, and the kids really felt it.

I walked around the Center after the meeting, speaking to different kids and introducing myself to some of the new ones. I always kept an eye out both in the planning book, which held a sheet with information, and on the floor for kids who might be involved in prostitution. Sometimes kids were so ashamed of admitting it that we never knew. Which meant we could never help them to deal with feelings of guilt and self-disgust. Often just watching how the boys and girls interacted with each other on the floor I could get an idea of how they had incorporated their sexuality as adolescents. Even those who had not had the experience of prostitution were extremely confused and conflicted about sexuality. It seemed to be a disease of our time.

I felt that adults who hadn't reached a certain degree of sexual honesty should not be working with these kids. I had hopes for a department devoted to human sexuality at the agency, to work in liaison with our medical staff. People to counsel prostitutes, both male and female, and youngsters who were experiencing sexual identity crises. The department would deal with victims of incest, transexualism, and transvestism, and could provide education on social diseases. Some of the staff were tired of hearing me talk about it. I suppose they thought I was obsessed with sex. I was—with healthy sex for all human beings.

I wanted to let the kids talk about and deal with their sexual feelings with enlightened, caring adults. Because I was an "ex-prostitute," my emphasis on this made some people very nervous. But I knew I had had a special experience which I could use to help these children. And though many of the staff had been open and willing to learn from my experience, to at least hear out my theories about what to do with these children, others were either condescending or simply ignored me. Some of the hard-heads acted like I was talking dirty when I brought it up. They had learned all they wanted to from social work tomes.

"Ms. Peterson, did my birth certificate come yet?" asked a tall black boy from Louisiana.

"No, Johnny, I didn't see any mail for you upstairs. Any luck job hunting?"

"Nope. Everybody wants someone experienced or educated," he said dejectedly.

"I think someone ought to take you to the clothing room and see if there's a sports jacket or suit that fits you." John was an extra mouth in an overpopulated, poor family. At seventeen he had left home to make it for himself and to lighten the load at home. He had no education, no skills, no family or friends in New York.

"Thanks, Ms. Peterson, I sure could use it."

35

I stopped and chatted with perhaps a dozen kids and was heading back upstairs when one of the volunteers caught me.

"What is it, Annie?" I asked her.

"It's Melissa. She's down at reception asking for you. She has big bruises on her face!"

I turned and flew down the stairs. In the reception area a small blond girl huddled in the chair. "Oh, Melissa, it's so good to see you!"

"I'm back," she said weakly, guiltily.

"C'mon, honey, let's get you upstairs. Annie, please get a change of clothes for Melissa, size five or smaller if you can find it, and meet us upstairs." Melissa had a shiny red tube top on, black satin shorts, black boots and a piteously thin silver jacket. There was a bruise on her left cheek that her makeup couldn't hide. Upstairs she took off her jacket and showed me her upper arms. Both were bruised and swollen.

"Oh, honey, you must be awfully sore. Who did this to you?"

She started crying. I sat beside her and took her in my arms. "Okay, honey, it's okay. You're safe now, ssh, okay." I rocked her back and forth. "We've been so worried about you! When you didn't come back at curfew that night I was really afraid the pimp had found you."

"I hate him! I'll kill him if he ever touches me again. I'm bleeding pretty bad and it hurts a lot," she moaned. "He stuck things up me till I bled, then made me go to work. I hate him!"

"My God, Melissa, we've got to get you to a doctor right away. How did he expect you to work, hurt and bleeding?"

"He said there was nothing wrong with my mouth!" she wailed.

"Oh sweetheart, Jesus, when did this happen?"

"Early this morning. Tonight I got one of my regular tricks to bring me here, 'cause he's been watching me every day, all the time!"

"Oh, Annie, good," I said, grabbing the clothes Annie had brought in. I helped Melissa to her feet.

"I can feel the blood. It's going to get all over!"

"Hang on, honey, we'll get you to the bathroom."

In the bathroom, Melissa sat weakly on the toilet seat, as I sat beside her on the tub holding her up. She was bleeding heavily and unnaturally. I was relieved when the nurse knocked on the door and came in. "I think we should get Melissa to a hospital right away," she said. "Call an ambulance."

When the ambulance squad arrived, Annie agreed to go with them. We bundled Melissa up and she went off on a stretcher. "Stay with her, Annie, please." Then I reminded Melissa not to worry, assuring her that Annie would tell the doctors about the pimp; that he wouldn't get into the hospital. "And I'll come and see you tomorrow, okay?" I tried to reassure the pale, still figure on the stretcher. She was so young and so small.

Somehow I got through the dinner hour. It was a terribly hectic time at the Center; eighty starving kids all trying to get their food first. Kids who hadn't eaten regularly and who, as one result, were often angry and hostile to any authority or adult. "This motherfucker stole my bread," etc. But we had to try to control the house. I made myself conspicuous, talking to the kids, de-escalating potential trouble whenever it sprang up.

At eight o'clock, when the Center seemed to be back in order, a staff member came in to tell me there were only thirty clean sheets.

"Oh damn! A sheet count's supposed to be done on the early shift! Well, I suppose they had emergencies too. We should have checked them earlier."

I turned then to the two maintenance men who'd just walked in. "Listen, guys, I've got some bad news. We need at least fifty more sheets for tonight." They both groaned. "Get a couple kids to give you a hand. One of you can start up the machines downstairs and the other one can take a detail of kids to the laundry. Let me get you some petty cash out of the safe." We needed the sheets by ten o'clock.

I left the men and found an available phone to call Annie at the hospital.

"Annie, what's happening down there?"

"Hi, Trudee. They're just checking Melissa into her room. They've stopped the bleeding. Did you know she was cut inside from glass? They're worried she might get a nasty infection, so they're starting her on antibiotics right away. She'll be all right but she's got to stay here. They called her mother and she hung up on them! Oh, and I told them about the pimp. They'll see that she's isolated and protected."

"Okay, thanks a lot. Annie, give her a kiss for me and tell her that I'll see her tomorrow afternoon. Bye."

I found Friar Bill in the basement standing in a mountain of sheets. "Bill, Melissa's gonna be all right, but she'll have to stay in the hospital a few days."

"Oh, that's good news. She really looked rough when she left here. Pimp?"

"Yeah, he really did her up this time, Bill. I'll spare you the grisly details, but the girl is in bad shape."

"Did they call her family?"

"Sure, but her mother said the same thing to them that she said to us when Melissa was here the first time: she doesn't want anything to do with the slut and she hangs up."

"I know. I read the file you wrote on her and tried to

38

understand what her mother felt but it's pretty hard to grasp. It's just not something you learn in seminary school."

"Oh, Bill, there should be more training on incest for people working in human services, but first people have to be willing to talk about it. Everybody is so afraid of it—keeping it in the closet—that it's dangerous."

"I just wasn't prepared for the feelings it aroused in me. First I was angry. Then, after I thought about it, it just made me sad."

"You see, Bill, Melissa's mother isn't strong enough to blame Melissa's father. She's afraid she'll lose him. She needs him more than Melissa, whatever he is."

"How could you adopt a kid and then abuse her like that?"

"If I knew that one, none of us would be here. She's been on the run from them since she was ten and they got her when she was eight and a half. She claims sexual abuse by her father and physical abuse by her mother, and I believe her, Bill."

"Boy, you wonder what kind of a chance she'll ever have."

"She's only thirteen; it depends on what happens in the next few years. If only she could get a really good family. Now I guess I'm dreaming. She's had forty placements in the last four years. Foster homes, group homes, detention, institutional schools, you name it, she's been there."

"I remember her file, it reads like a horror story. How did you ever get her to tell you all that?"

"Well, she's been here twice now, and I spent a lot of time with her both times. I also told her about my own involvement with prostitution. She opened up more after that. I guess she didn't feel so ashamed when she knew that I'd had some of the same experiences. She still doesn't talk much, she's very antagonistic, untrusting. I really can't blame her."

Annie was up in the office with Melissa's file before her. "Hi, how are you doing?" I asked her. "You look tired."

"I am beat. That emergency room really tired me out. But Melissa was sleeping like a baby when I left."

"She really is still a child. Sexual sophistication is all she has. Poor little thing can probably do it fifty different ways but she's still a baby underneath. That's the real horror of it."

"Did you know it's her birthday tomorrow?" Annie asked. "I just noticed that she'll be fourteen tomorrow."

"My God, some birthday present that pimp gave her." Suddenly I sat down, almost in tears.

"Are you okay?" Annie asked.

"Oh, Annie, I'll never understand why children have to live like this. At least she's alive, I still have a chance to help her."

"I know, Trudee. I heard that one of your girls was found dead. I'm really sorry. Apparently Melissa feels very good about you. She asked for you twice tonight, she said you *knew* about her."

"I know," I said with a sigh. "If only I could work with her a longer time, maybe I would have a chance to really help. Annie, I swear on Heather's dead body, I'll work harder. I swear it! I wish I could take Melissa home and just start her upbringing over again!"

"I feel that way about certain kids, too."

"It's unprofessional, but I still wish I could. Well, I better get ready to take casework update. It's almost ten o'clock. Thanks again, Annie."

"Ms. Peterson," a voice called out to me as I came

down the stairs. "I need my medication." It was a nineteen-year-old boy who had been in more psychiatric institutions than any kid I knew. He lived in three months, and out three, then in for three more. He took Thorazine and probably would all his life.

"Okay," I told him, "ask the nurse to come in, she's in charge of meds tonight."

"Okay, Ms. Peterson."

I took casework update from the staff and while staff organized bedding I called the administrator to give the evening's update. The next shift started arriving and assuming the running of the house. By the time I finished my paperwork it was 12:45. I called the hospital, and found out that Melissa was resting comfortably. So is Heather, I thought. No more pain, no more degradation.

I sank into the back seat of the taxi on the way uptown. (I couldn't bring myself to go onto the subway late at night. I knew that scene only too well.) The quiet felt good now. I was almost too tired to think. That was good.

My own kids, Joe and Jess, were sleeping soundly when I came in. I tiptoed into the bedroom where Jessie lay curled up in a fetal ball. I thought, Melissa's even younger than Jessie, and Jessie's only fifteen. And Heather was just a few years older. I kneeled by Jessie and stroked her hair for a moment.

When I finally got into bed and fell asleep, my dreams brought me to a start. Melissa and Jessie and Heather were all one person: interchangeable, dying, bleeding, arms and legs severed. It was me, then them again. A maniac's body looming over us-me-them stroking himself. It was 6 A.M., but I wouldn't go back to sleep. What was Heather's killer doing now? Did he have trouble sleeping, too?

* * *

"Pediatrics, please." Here I am calling a girl who's slept with hundreds of old men—in Pediatrics! How bizarre. "Hello, my name is Trudee Peterson. I work at the Center where Melissa Roberts was staying. How is she this morning? . . . Thanks. By the way, it's her birthday today and she really doesn't have much family. Maybe you could tell the other nurses. . . . Thanks a lot. Goodbye."

Later, I arrived at the hospital ready to comfort and encourage Melissa. I stopped at the nurses' station and asked them to inform Melissa's doctor and the hospital social worker that I was available.

"Hi, sweetheart. Happy birthday!"

"Hi. How did you know it was my birthday?" she said shyly.

I wanted to preserve that moment and the expression on her face for all eternity. The surprise, pleasure, innocence, and beauty caught my heart and tore it open. In the white hospital gown, her thin frame looked even younger.

"Well, your birthdate is on your file and Annie reminded me last night. There was no way I was gonna miss it!" I set my packages down and gave her a careful hug. "Happy birthday, honey."

Her eyes shone with pleasure and joy. It takes so little to make her feel good, I thought, she's so rarely gotten what she deserved.

"Oh, I like it," she squealed when she took the

nightgown out of the wrapper, "Thank you. This hospital job is really ugly."

Her eyes filled with tears when she opened the second gift: a silver chain.

"Oh, it's so pretty." The gratitude in her eyes made me turn away. I busied myself with the cake.

"Hope you like chocolate," I said as I put fourteen yellow candles on it.

"What's this, a party and no one invited me?" a nurse said who'd just walked in. "Just a minute, don't light it yet," she said as she disappeared again.

She came back in a few moments with a crew of two nurses, an aide, and an intern.

As I lit the candles Melissa started to cry quietly. It did seem strange for this group of people to be singing "Happy Birthday" to an abused, lonely child in an antiseptic white hospital bed. A testament to what modern life was doing to people.

We got very cozy in the room after the nurses resumed their duties. Melissa was both sad and happy from the effect of the kindness around her, and she opened up to me more than ever before.

"Do you remember where you lived before you went to the orphanage?" I asked.

"I was sent to the orphanage when I was four. I think that was in Washington, because that's where I was born, near Seattle. After a while I went on a plane to California. I was really small. They were mean at the orphanage."

"How long did you stay in California?"

"Not very long. A lady came and got me. She was nice. She took me on a plane again. That must have been when I went to Connecticut. I guess I was about six then. I was in two homes before I ended up at the Jameses house. I think one of them was going to adopt me, but they changed their mind. I don't know why. They were very nice to me, I liked it there," she said wistfully. The pain of that rejection still hung there in her eyes.

"Let me fix your pillows, you're all lopsided," I said, using this excuse to comfort her. I fluffed the pillows and straightened out the bedding.

"I left there," she continued, "and stayed in another house with a lot of foster kids. It was a big house and the kids were mean, the older kids. I hated it there." Her dark eyes looked almost black. "Then finally the Jameses adopted me. Big deal, I really hate them, I'll never go back there again!"

"You won't have to, honey, the State of Connecticut has charge of you now. What happened when you left the Jameses?"

"They put me in another foster home. I only stayed three days and ran away again."

"Why?"

"I didn't like it. I was in lots of places after that, I kept running. Sometimes they didn't catch me for a couple of weeks. One group home I liked and I stayed there for six months. That was a long time!"

"And what happened to that?"

"I don't know, it closed and we all had to leave. The house parents were nice though. I think I went to the residential school after that, then I came to New York when I ran away from that."

"How did you meet your pimp?"

"At an after-hours club."

"How did a thirteen-year-old girl find an after-hours club?"

"Easy. I met somebody on the Deuce and he took me there. I wasn't in there an hour before he had me. I never saw the other guy again."

"Is it possible he sold you to the pimp?"

"I guess so. But he told me I could stay with him and his wife!" she said. "He didn't bother me for a few days and his old lady was good to me at first. She got me a bunch of new clothes, I felt really good, grown up, like. Then . . . they got really nasty. It surprised me, I was confused by the way they started acting. They said I owed them a bunch of money for taking care of me. When I offered to leave them, and the new clothes, he hit me, then he raped me in front of her. Evil bitch just sat in a chair when I was screaming, filing her nails." She turned and looked out the window.

"I'm sorry people have hurt you, Melissa. I know there are plenty of evil, sick people in the world but not everyone is like that."

"I went to work that night," she said, ignoring what I'd said. "I got used to 'the life.' It's all I know how to do now."

"Honey, you're just fourteen, there's lots of things you can still learn to do."

"I'm not going back to Connecticut, ever!" she said vehemently.

"How about coming back to the Center when you're better and we'll see if we can get you funded out of state, I mean out of Connecticut. Maybe you could get placed in New York. Would you want that?"

"I don't know. I'm tired of being placed."

"I can appreciate that, Melissa, but it's just too hard to survive on your own at your age. You get hurt too much."

"I get hurt when I get placed too."

"I know you have, honey, but if I get you placed I'll make sure it's a good place and we can keep in touch."

"Really, you think you could do that?" she asked skeptically.

"Well, I'd try, though I can't promise anything. I'll tell you what, if they refuse placement, you know the Center isn't locked. You can always split. But I don't think you should."

"I don't know." She sounded tired and confused.

"I think I better let you rest for a while, you look like you're worn out. I'll come back tomorrow, okay?"

"Okay, thanks for coming and for the cake and everything." She looked even lonelier now that she'd found a friend to talk to.

"Honey, I know adults haven't been too good to you, but like I said, we're not all alike and I'd really like to be with you. I want to be your friend. I've lived through a lot of the same things you have. Tomorrow I'll tell you more about my life. It's not a very pretty story either, but I survived it, and I bet you can, too. You've got a lot of strength for someone so young, and a lot of goodness, too. Maybe I can help you learn that."

I put my arms around her, and for just a moment she snuggled into them, then pulled away shyly. "There is something I'd like to have when you come tomorrow."

"Anything but cigarettes!"

"No, I don't have to smoke. I would like a pad to draw on."

"Oh, I didn't know you were an artist! Of course I'll get you one. I'll be here with it as soon as visiting hours start, okay?"

"Bye, thanks for coming."

"Goodbye, sweetheart," I said as I kissed her cheek. Her eyes clung to me as I left the room.

At the nurses' station I ran into the resident physician assigned to Melissa's case. I introduced myself, and he asked if I could give him some information. We sat in the empty waiting room, where I gratefully lit a cigarette. Then I told him everything I knew about

Melissa's background, and he suggested I speak to the social worker there as well. I did, and after a long discussion, I told the social worker I'd appreciate any help she might be able to give me in getting Melissa funded in New York.

"She's just going to run from any place they put her in Connecticut," I insisted. "If we could keep her in New York, I could continue to work with her. She trusts me a little bit. Look, if she keeps running and living on the streets, this kid's gonna wind up a statistic!" Like Heather.

"You don't have to convince me," she said. "I think it's a good idea. And she really thinks a lot of you."

"I'm sorry. I feel like I'm preparing for the battle," I apologized. "I know it's going to be some fight to get her funded here."

This social worker was clearly sympathetic. She said, "One thing I could do is to get a psychiatrist to see Melissa. Maybe we could get some support that way."

Not a bad idea, I thought. I said I would discuss it with Melissa the next day.

Things were no more placid than usual when I got to the Center. The meat for dinner wasn't defrosted— they'd taken it out too late.

I searched the face of the volunteer cook. "Can you make chicken à la king? There's some canned chicken downstairs and we've got all those donated biscuits from the bakery."

"I don't know. I've never made it for eighty people," he said.

"I'll find someone to help you out."

Why did these things always happen on my shift?

A staff member came up and asked me, "Ms. Peterson, who's on intake tonight?"

"Why, you got somebody?"

"Two kids from Puerto Rico, who don't speak any English."

"Shit," I said, throwing my pencil down. "I don't think we have any Spanish-speaking counselors on tonight. Ask one of the Spanish-speaking residents to get the basics. Ask them if they want food and a shower first and tell them no drugs and no fighting."

I picked up my pencil again and started to write. The phone rang immediately.

"Trudee, I've got a girl on the line. She won't come in, she sounds suicidal. I think you better talk to her."

"Put her through."

"Hello," a quiet voice said.

"Hi, I'm Trudee, what's your name?"

Not a sound at the other end.

"You don't have to tell me your name, honey. It's okay, we can just talk."

Nothing.

"Are you there?"

"Yes."

"Can you tell me what's wrong?"

"My father."

"What about him, honey?"

"He does things to me," she said, crying softly.

"Does he hurt you?"

"No, you mean hit me?"

"I mean in any way."

"The things he does are driving me crazy!"

"Is it sexual?"

"How did you know?"

48

"How old are you, honey?"

"Twelve."

"Does your mother live with you?"

"Uh huh. She's sick."

"Do you have an aunt or uncle that you're close to?"

"They don't live in New Jersey. They live in other states."

"Would you like to come here?"

The door opened and a counselor announced that there was a fight downstairs.

"Honey, don't go away, please. Okay? Don't go away. I'm going to leave the phone for a few minutes, okay?"

"Okay."

I put the call on hold and ran down the steps. Two boys were on the floor scuffling and two counselors were pulling them apart. I stepped between the boys as they got to their feet.

"He got my money," one of them screamed.

"You fucking fag, you're a liar!"

"Take Jerry into the office, please," I directed the counselor who was holding the boy.

"C'mon upstairs with me, Mike," I said to the other boy.

"I didn't take his fucking money. Goddamn fag wants to start trouble."

"We don't talk like that here, Mike."

"Fuck you, you white bitch. What do you know?"

"Well, I know you can't talk like that and stay here." The boy pushed past me and headed for the door. "You can all go to hell," he shouted.

"If you want to talk when you calm down, we'll still be here," I called after him as he slammed out the door. I went to the receptionist and told him not to let Mike in for twenty-four hours. "I'll talk to him if he wants to talk it through, but only if he's willing to do it calmly."

Back upstairs, I picked up the phone and the line was dead. Damn, I should have given the call to someone else. Damn. I prayed she'd call back.

Someone came running in to tell me that a Puerto Rican girl had arrived, apparently ill. I hurried over to the couch where she'd been put. "It's Iris Cortes," I said. "Bill, get the kids downstairs and watch for the ambulance. Have them come in the side door. Annie, you help Bill, and somebody get me some cold towels!"

"We found her on Forty-second and Eighth Avenue," one of the boys told me excitedly.

"I'm glad you brought her in. Do you know what happened?"

"No, she was just lying there. People were stepping over her, so we picked her up and brought her!"

"Iris, Iris," I said to the immobile body. I felt her pulse. It seemed weak. "Iris. *Mira, mira,* Iris, *despuerta, despuerta,*" I said, hoping I had the right word for wake up.

She opened her eyes and her long lashes fluttered. I picked her up and took off her coat. Her arms were clean, no tracks. "It must be some kind of pills," I said. I wiped her face lightly with the cold towels and her eyes fluttered again. She mumbled something in Spanish. "Where's Bill? He speaks a little Spanish." I sent one of the kids downstairs for him. "I only wish I understood!"

Before we could bring her around the ambulance arrived and took her away.

"Trudee, telephone," Annie called. "It's one of your kids, I think."

"Hello?"

"Ma, Joey won't leave me alone and I'm tired of it! I hate him!" Jessie said on the other end.

50

"Let me speak to him, Jess," I said, exhausted.

"If he doesn't leave me alone, I'm leaving. I can't live with him!"

Annie came back over and tapped me on the shoulder. "There's a call for you on the other line, Trudee. I think it's Wayne, from the Runaway Squad." She was beginning to sound weary herself.

Oh my God, I thought. He must be calling about Delia. "Please tell him I'll call him right back," I told Annie.

Joey's voice hit my ear. "Ma, I'm not gonna take her shit. She's not my mother. I'm sick of her trying to boss me around!"

"What did she do, Joe?"

"She just tries to order me around, and she can't!" he said angrily.

"Joey, I've got a couple of emergencies here myself. Why don't you both go to bed and we'll talk about it tomorrow."

I hung up, offering a little prayer that those children of mine who had been through so much with me would make it through tonight too and let me talk some sense into them in the morning. They were terrific and understood perfectly the work I was doing, but it was still a strain having me out of the house so much.

Before returning Wayne's call—which I was dreading—I took a few moments to compose myself on the subject of Delia Liston.

Delia had first appeared at the Center several months

ago. I had just barely gotten that night's crew in to dinner when someone came to tell me that I was needed upstairs immediately. I went straight to my office. The door was closed, but through the glass I could see Jimmy Kelly, another supervisor, speaking intensely to a beautiful girl of about fifteen. Her hair was long and brown and in considerable disarray. She had on a typical outfit: a red bodysuit and short black shorts over red Spandex pants and pointy silver boots.

Jimmy motioned me in. "Trudee, I'd like you to meet Delia Liston," he said. "Delia, Trudee is the supervisor on duty now. You might like to talk to her."

"Hi, Delia," I said, offering my hand.

She turned and looked out the window—but not before she could throw me a cold and resentful glare. Jimmy and I exchanged a look; we were both saddened by her hostility and fear.

"Okay, Dee," Jimmy said, "you can go eat now and shower afterward. You know where the bathrooms are, don't you?"

She gave us each another dirty look and sauntered out of the office.

"Okay, Jimmy, shoot," I said when she was out of earshot.

"Age fifteen . . ."

I was getting pretty good at spotting how old they were, I realized.

". . . from upstate New York, working-class family. She's run away about six times, won't say too much about her home life. Obviously, it's not too good. She goes into hustling every time she runs away. She hasn't got a pimp."

My eyebrows rose as I looked up from Delia's file. "That's amazing. How can she work these streets alone?"

"She doesn't. She works in a house in the Twenties on the West Side."

"Aha, smart girl." I laughed. "She doesn't seem very pleased about being here. What's the story?"

Jimmy explained that the Runaway Squad had brought her. He was very concerned. "I don't know if she'll stay, Trudee. Try and get to her, talk to her, will you? She needs help badly but she won't accept it. She's very closed."

"I'll give it my best, Jimmy," I assured him, though I already had my doubts about what lay behind those eyes. "Hey, you better get out of here. Your shift ended three hours ago!"

I found Delia coming out of the bathroom after dinner. Her long hair was brushed and softly curling now. She had changed into warm blue corduroys and a sweater. The difference was remarkable.

"Uh, where do I put the dirty towels?" she asked in bitter patience.

"Over here on the machine," I said, leading her to the doors that hid the washer and dryer.

"Will I get my shit back?"

"Yes, of course," I said, hoping she would. Stealing in the Center was extremely difficult to control. "Will you come sit and talk with me?"

"What about?" she asked suspiciously.

"Oh, about you, and me, and life."

"I have nothing to say."

"Well, maybe you could listen to me."

"I'm not staying, you can't keep me here," she said, grabbing her clothes off the washer. She put on her coat and headed for the stairway.

I went after her. "Why don't you stay, Delia, at least till your hair dries. You'll get sick going out like that."

"I can take care of myself."

I had to keep trying. "Please stay, Dee, you're really welcome here. I'd like to help. I've had a lot of experience too, the same things you're going through now. Let me help. Just talk to me, honey."

"No, I'm leaving," she said obstinately, pushing past me.

"Delia, it's a miserable life, it's very hurtful for you to have to sleep with so many men and give yourself to them hour after hour, day after day. Giving blow jobs to old men is a wretched life for anyone, much less a young girl!"

At these last words she turned and stared at me hard, and for a moment her eyes softened.

"Leave me alone!" she yelled, hurrying down the stairs.

"Delia, I'll always be here if you change your mind," I called in a last attempt.

She was gone. I watched out the window and saw her scurry into the crowds and on into 42nd Street. Damn.

I called the Runaway Squad and told them she'd taken off. Now they'd have to put her in Spofford when they picked her up next time, so she wouldn't be able to run away again. At least she wasn't working in the streets.

She was safer than Heather had been.

*　　*　　*

Two weeks after Delia Liston walked out she walked back in, this time of her own accord.

"You said you'd talk to me anytime," she said grudgingly.

"Yes, of course, Delia. I'm awfully glad to see you," I said warmly. I was truly delighted that she had come back.

"I stopped by a few days ago but you weren't here."

"Well, I'm here now. Let's go someplace to talk."

We found an empty room and sat down facing each other.

"You said we could talk about things if I wanted to."

"Yes, of course. What's wrong?"

"It's the tricks, I don't think I can take it much longer."

"Can you go home?"

"NO! I'm *not* going home!" she said forcefully.

"Okay, okay," I reassured her. "What would you like to do?"

"Get a straight job and stay in New York."

"Is that realistic, Dee? You haven't got an education, what kind of a job could you get?"

"Waitress or something. Don't you have job counselors here?"

"Yes, we do, but the first thing they'll tell you is to finish your school." I hardly paused before taking the next plunge. "Tell me a little bit about your home, Dee?"

She made an unpleasant face. "There's nothing to tell," she said flatly.

"Well, why won't you go there?"

"I don't like it."

We went on this way for many sessions. She continued to come in, but she refused to allow me to contact her mother and she wouldn't stay at the

Center. Still, the sporadic counseling was a beginning.

I finally called Wayne, my friend and contact at the Runaway Squad.

"Have you ever spoken to Delia Liston's parents?" I asked him.

"Yes," he told me. "That time when she was picked up and taken over to you. I spoke to her mother. She sounded very nice on the phone, said she just couldn't understand why Dee wouldn't stay home. She made everything sound normal and homey. But you know I rarely trust that. Why would Delia be where she is today? The father works in a warehouse, doesn't seem to be involved too much with raising the kids—there're two other kids younger than Delia at home."

"Well, that doesn't give us much," I said. "She refuses to talk about them, becomes a mute whenever they're brought up. I can't contact them because she won't give permission and she's not staying here. I'm afraid if I get to them and she finds out, she'll stop coming to see me, and I think she really needs me right now."

Wayne read my mind. "I could contact them," he said, "and tell them you've been working with her and ask the mother to call you. I don't need permission and I won't be breaking a trust."

I grinned as I hung up, feeling just a little devious. I comforted myself with the fact that I was doing it for her. Something was keeping her out of that house, and I couldn't help unless I knew what. She was relatively safe working in that brothel, but what it was doing to her head was devastating. Dee hated herself for every trick that she allowed to crawl on top of her, and in between, when she sat waiting for them to come. She should have been carrying her school books and having Cokes after school with boys she liked, not asking old men if they wanted a French or a straight and making sure she had a supply of rubbers sufficient for the day's work. I hated her life for her, and knew she hated it too.

One evening when I came on duty I noticed Delia sleeping on the pillows on the floor of the Center. She was curled up into a little ball.

"When did she come in?" I asked Rick.

"Yesterday," he told me. "She's been sleeping a lot."

"Probably exhausted. Or maybe it's just escape sleeping," I said, as much to myself as to Rick. "She looks rough."

He nodded. "They always do."

I leaned down and touched her hair. "Let her sleep. I'll talk to her later."

Before long, Delia appeared at the door to my office, rubbing her eyes.

"I've been wanting to talk to you," she mumbled.

"I'm sorry I wasn't here when you came in, honey. Come sit down. What is it, Dee?"

"I had a really bad trick the other night. It freaked me out."

"What happened?"

"He . . . asked me to do something. I'm not sure what happened really 'cause he gave me some pills."

"Where were you?"

Someone knocked on the door. I opened it a crack. "I'm sorry, Trudee, but I've got to get some medication," one of the volunteers said.

"It's okay, c'mon in."

Delia turned and looked out the window. She watched the action on the street sadly. The phone rang and I set up an appointment as quickly as I could.

"I'm sorry, babe."

"It's okay. I know you're busy," she said, hanging her head.

"Not too busy for you. Now what about this trick, what kind of pills did he give you?"

"I don't know. I know it sounds dumb of me to take them, but I just wanted to get high. Well, before I started feeling high, he, uh, asked me to do some things. I told him no way. Then I woke up in his place, I must have passed out. I don't know what happened."

"Where was he?"

"I don't know. He wasn't there. It was strange, because there was hardly anything in the apartment. Just some furniture. No clothes or food or anything. I got up and left."

"Do you want to talk about what he wanted you to do?"

The office door swung open and we were interrupted again, this time by another volunteer dropping off some files. I tried not to let my attention be distracted from Delia.

"It's just that it really makes me scared," she said. "I couldn't wait to talk to you. Now, well, I guess it's hard to say."

"Whatever you want, honey," I said stroking her arm.

"I feel so ugly. He wanted me to . . . to. . . . Well, damn, I feel so ugly!"

"Take it easy, honey."

The phone rang again. Damn. "Trudee Peterson."

It was the switchboard. "Trudee, the two volunteers from Long Island won't be in tonight. They just called in and said they were sorry."

"Okay, thanks. Listen, could you hold my calls for a while? Unless it's something urgent, okay?"

Delia sighed and put her hands over her face. The

street noises drifted into the room.

"He wanted me to go to the bathroom on him!" She spat the words out.

"Oh, Dee, oh honey." I kissed her hair and put my arm around her.

"I've been feeling so disgusted and sick. I was high for three days and then I just wanted to talk to you and you weren't here."

"I'm so sorry, honey."

"Boy, I must be the lowest thing in the world for some guy to ask me to do that."

"Oh no, it's not you, it's him. He's the one who's sick."

"Why did he ask me to do that?" She shuddered.

"I guess I just don't know what makes some people the way they are. Other girls have told me about tricks like that. I just don't know."

"Do you think . . . do you think, he could have made me do that when I was passed out?"

"I doubt it very much. Maybe he got off just saying it to you. Maybe that's why he left, because he didn't want to face you. Delia, honey, please stay this time. Please leave 'the life.' It's too hard on you, honey, it'll kill you. Please, please leave it."

"Maybe I'll go home and deal with the bastard."

So, here it comes, I thought. I didn't have to bother setting Wayne up, after all.

Delia kept on. "It's always men, tricks or fathers or whatever."

"I know you probably won't believe me," I said gently, "but not all the men in the world are like the tricks you see, or your father. Someday you'll meet some nice men, but certainly not where you've been living right now."

"Right, nice ones, sure. Well, I wanted to talk to

somebody so bad, to tell somebody about all that. But you were the only one I could say it to, you know. It's so ugly."

"I understand, Dee, and I'm sorry I wasn't here when you came in yesterday. Please leave the streets, honey, please."

"Is it okay if I stay a few days with you?"

"Absolutely."

"Will you be here?"

"I'm on for the next four days."

"Then I'll stay. I knew you would be okay about it. I mean not look at me like I was some kind of monster," she said, looking up at me.

"Oh, honey, you're not a monster," I said, smoothing her hair back.

She did stay those four days, and then she left again. I never did hear any more about her father either.

Then one day, there she was again. She sat with me on the window sill, staring at the street. Her pretty face was framed against the filth and the midtown hustlers passing by outside.

"I called my mother yesterday."

"Uh huh." I nodded quietly, hoping she'd let some more out this time.

"I think I'll go home for a while," she said softly. "My ma says my little sister has been getting into things. I better go straighten her out." She was pensive, more serious than I had ever seen her.

"I think it's great that you want to help her. She's lucky to have you."

Delia gave me a "Yeah, right" look and said, "She's just a kid."

I couldn't laugh at Dee—a fifteen-year-old saying this, because it wasn't funny. There wasn't much kid left in Dee.

"What will happen when you go home, Dee?"

"Oh, my old man will probably give me a beating and my ma will cry and then I'll only take so much for so long and try to kill my old man again."

"'Again'?"

Dee was silent. She seemed to look through me. "Yeah well, I just thought I'd say goodbye."

"I'm really glad you did. Delia," I said, touching her arm, "if you need anything when you're there or if you just want to talk, please call me."

She pulled away and started for the door. "I'm gay you know," she said defiantly, turning, waiting for my response.

"That doesn't mean I can't touch you, does it?" I asked.

Her face relaxed a little, almost turning into a smile. "Bye," she said.

"Goodbye, Delia, you know where to find me."

And she was gone.

Now I felt I had to call Wayne again. I told him Delia was going home. He told me that he had in fact spoken with Delia's mother again and that she had told him she would get in touch with me.

"She never did," I said, "unless I didn't get the message—which is entirely possible around here. What else did she say?"

"That's all. I told her you were working with Dee. How is she?"

"I don't know, Wayne, not too hot I'd guess. She said her old man would probably beat her when she got there."

"I'm sure. I had a talk with the caseworker from children's services who tried to place Dee a couple years ago. The father is pretty abusive to the whole family. Guess he's alcoholic. Dee ran before she could be placed."

"Well, things are starting to fall into place, she's beginning to talk to me a little more. She drops in, on an irregular basis, but she keeps dropping in." I was hopeful.

But I had heard nothing further about Delia. Now Wayne was calling me. I certainly couldn't put off returning his call, but I couldn't pretend I wasn't scared of what he might have to tell me.

"Hello, Wayne?" I had my fingers crossed.

"Hi, Trudee. Do you know anything about Delia Liston?"

Here goes, I thought. "No. What's happened?"

"Well, it seems Delia's father beat her pretty bad. She was taken to the hospital."

"Oh, no. Is she all right?"

Wayne was reassuring. "I think so," he said. "Physically, at least. She took off from the hospital last night. They were holding her for a few days' observation. She had some pretty bad bruises and they were worried about a concussion. But the x-rays came out okay. I'm just worried about where her head's at, what she'll do now. I thought she'd contact you."

"No, I wish she would. It doesn't seem likely she'd go to work in that condition. Why did he beat her up? Or is that a stupid question?"

"The father was waving a gun around, threatening to shoot the mother and all the kids. Guess it was a pretty nasty scene."

I gasped.

62

"Get this. Delia tackled him, and got the gun away. The other kids ran with the gun, but Delia stayed and took the beating so her mother wouldn't have to. Mess, huh?"

"Poor Dee. Jesus, what we do to our kids."

"I thought you should know. I'll keep an eye out for her too."

"Thanks a lot for letting me know, Wayne."

I put the phone down. But before I could think for a minute about Delia, it rang again. "Trudee Peterson speaking."

"Hello, this is Mirta Cortes, I hear my niece was there and somebody call my house but I no here."

"Mrs. Cortes, is Iris your niece?"

"*Si.* What is matter? That girl so wild nobody can take care her since her mama die. She no mind nobody. I don't know how to do for her. I got other kids too, you know, and—"

"Mrs. Cortes," I interrupted. "Iris was taken to the hospital. We don't know what's wrong. Maybe somebody gave her some pills or something. She's at Saint Vincent's."

The woman started to cry. I gave her the number and encouraged her to go to the hospital.

Then my mind went back to Delia. If only I could will her to come in so I could help her with the pain . . .

"Trudee. There's a case I'd like to talk to you about," Rick said, snapping me back to tonight at this busy Center. I knew I couldn't do anything for Delia unless she presented herself here.

"It's a boy. I know you've worked mostly with girls, but I think you're the best one for this."

Of course I was willing, but I didn't know how comfortable the boy would be with me. "It may be hard for him to talk to a woman. He's been into 'the life'?"

63

"Yes, and pretty heavy," Rick said. "He's feeling real bad about himself. Maybe even suicidal. Will you at least try to talk to him?"

I sighed. Another one. At best I could probably give him twenty minutes. How the hell could I do anything for him in twenty minutes? "What's his name?"

"Martin Elkins. He's from the Midwest somewhere—Ohio, I think. He's been in New York six or eight months. He's sixteen."

Same old story. "He works for a pimp or is he on his own?"

"He got mixed up with a pimp when he first came here, but got away. He's been working over in the Fifties on the East Side on his own."

I knew that strip. The young boys came out of the woodwork at night. There were eleven- and twelve-year-old boys—"chickens"—working over there. All male customers: "chickenhawks."

"Okay. Introduce me," I said, "and then you get on home."

The boy sat alone ignoring the general chaos of the other kids. He was staring at his hands, rubbing them together.

"Marty?" Rick said.

The boy looked up. He had a beautiful face, delicate and intense. Blond curls made him look almost like a cherub.

"This is Trudee Peterson. We talked about her last night when you came in."

"Hi, Marty," I said, sitting down on the pillow beside him.

"Hi," he said despondently.

"I'd like to talk to you sometime, okay?"

"Now?" he asked hopefully.

"Sure," I said. This one wasn't at all reluctant to tell

me his sad and painful story. He needed desperately to spill out the ugliness. We went up to the office.

". . . So when my foster parents found out I was gay, they didn't throw me out. They each dealt with it in a different way. My mother sent me to a psychiatrist. He seduced me," he said bitterly. "My father never spoke to me again. It was like being invisible."

"How old were you when they found out?"

"Thirteen, almost fourteen. When I realized I was different, I didn't know what to do about it. I was scared. I wanted to talk to somebody so bad," he said sadly.

"Did you tell your mother what the psychiatrist did?"

"No, I couldn't. She had such high hopes. She was sure I would get over it. Since she was the only one talking to me, I was afraid of losing her, and I thought that if I told her she'd think it was my fault. Then she'd stop talking to me too. I just didn't go back, and he never told my mother. It was really confusing because she never asked about why he didn't send any more bills. I wanted her to ask, but I was afraid to bring it up."

"Were you angry?"

He looked surprised. "Not then, I don't think." He paused. "But I was later, now that I think about it."

"Well, you certainly had a right to be."

"My mother never referred to it again, like it didn't exist. When I finally had the courage to bring it up, she changed the subject and told me she was sure I'd be okay."

"That's a loaded comment," I pointed out. "As if you weren't okay, right?"

"Definitely." He nodded. "The hardest part was my father, though. I'd been with them since I was four, and I thought we were close. Like he used to do things with me, fishing and stuff. I loved that. When I tried to talk to him, he'd leave the room or nod or shake his head. My mother just kept chattering like everything was fine. It was awful."

"It must have been very painful to be denied your father's caring."

"It was," he said quietly, near tears. "I loved him."

"And you don't now?"

"I don't know how I feel about them. I keep remembering how it was before."

"Do you feel like you're responsible?"

"Well, I guess so. If I hadn't been gay it would have been all right."

"Did you get gay on purpose?"

"No," he said, looking at me strangely.

"Then you couldn't help it, right?"

"But they acted as though I had disappointed them. I guess I did."

"You didn't do anything on purpose, Marty. They may have been unable to deal with who you were out of fear and ignorance, but you didn't sit down one day and decide, 'Well, I think I'll be gay. That will really hurt my parents.'"

He gave me a half smile. "I know, but . . . it sure would have been better if I was straight. I tried to be. I took girls to the movies and a few school dances, but I just didn't want to touch them." He looked ashamed. "I had a friend, all he could talk about was getting into some girl's jeans and all I thought about was getting into his." This time he did smile, weakly.

I smiled back, saying, "I can see how that would be a problem. Did you?"

"No. I finally got the courage to try though. We used to mess around a little bit sexually." He started to blush. "Like masturbate together and stuff like that. Then one time I tried to kiss him and he called me a queer and a faggot. He was right. He didn't hang out with me any more, and he told a lot of kids at school."

"Marty, you're a human being," I said, touching his hand, "and you seem like a very nice one."

"'Wish my parents thought so. I left home after the incident with Doug—that was his name. I had about three hundred fifty dollars saved from my part-time job and I got a bus ticket to New York."

"The land of milk and honey, right?"

"Yeah." He smiled sadly. "This guy I knew from home, told me that he'd been here, and there was a lot of action. 'You can probably get into male modeling with no problem at all,' he said. The first thing I met out here was a pimp," he said venomously. "He was a rotten son-of-a-bitch."

"Most of them are."

"I didn't even really know about pimps, not really. I had no idea that's what he was when he picked me up outside the bus station. I wasn't in New York twenty minutes!" he said, still incredulous that it had happened to him. "Boy, was I dumb!"

"Honey, thousands of kids are picked up the same way all over the country," I told him. "I don't think they, or you, are dumb, just innocent, naive. If you're not *aware* of something, you can't *beware* of it."

Marty was hardly listening. He had so much to get out. "He was really mean to me, to all of us. He had five boys. He brought his friends over when we finished work and they'd come over all coked up and, well, you know. If any of the boys cried he'd beat them. There was one boy only twelve. I think I felt worse for him than for me," he said, hanging his head.

"How long were you there?" I asked quietly.

"Almost five months." He sighed and leaned back against the wall. "I was so scared of him. I thought he'd kill me if I left him. I just knew he'd catch me. We were *all* scared. He never talked to us, but snarled, kind of. I don't know what made him so fucking mean but— Ms. Peterson, Rick told me you had been, uh, in 'the life' too. Was it painful for you?"

"Very, Marty. Very painful," I said gravely.

"How did you get over it, or did you?" he said begging me with his eyes to tell him it would go away.

"I won't lie to you, Marty. I don't think it ever leaves entirely. But you can use it in constructive ways. I learned a lot about human beings and pain and loneliness, and I use it to help people, including myself. See, when I help someone leave that life, it's kind of therapy for me, do you understand?"

"I think so. I guess it takes a long time?"

"It depends how hard you work at it."

"When I left the pimp—"

"Wait," I interrupted. "How did you get away?"

"I stayed with one of my tricks out in New Jersey for a few days. But he was a professor and said he couldn't let me stay too long or somebody would find out. He gave me enough money to get a room for a week. I hustled for a while out there, but that was hard. Finally, I called a pizza place where one of the boys used to hang out and talked to him. He said our pimp had been arrested on a gun charge, and all the boys had scattered so none of the other pimps would move in. Then I came back and stayed with him for a while. I guess I've been lucky. I just stay away from the hotels and clubs where the guy's friends go."

"So you've been working independently for a few months?"

He nodded.

"What made you come here, Marty?"

"I don't know. I heard someone mention it." His voice trailed off. I sat holding his hands, saying nothing. I felt he had more to say to me.

Finally, he blurted out, "I just can't take it any more." He began to weep. "You know, they lay the thirty dollars on the dresser and walk away and never hold you or give you any affection. It's so cold and lonely. Is it too much to ask, just to be held for a minute? And you can't have a relationship with anybody. If I wasn't young, they wouldn't want me anyway." He was sobbing. "You know, some of the tricks have actually told me I'm too old! Wow, washed up before I'm seventeen!" He laughed sarcastically through his tears.

I put my arms around him, and he dropped his head to my shoulder and cried. "I'm sorry, Marty. I'm sorry," I whispered. Then, after a few minutes, I said, "Marty, I think you're going to make it. You're sensitive yet strong. That's what it takes. Let me help you."

"Okay," he said softly, tiredly. He was young, just a boy. Oh God, they were all so young.

I stayed till three o'clock in the morning talking to Jimmy Kelly after the Center quieted down. We called the hospital and found out that Iris Cortes was doing all right. It helped to talk things over with Jimmy. Sometimes the tension from a night like this had to be dealt with before you went home. That's how staff helped each other. If there was time.

I crawled from the cab to my house to bed. Before I passed out, I thanked God that Iris was alive and asked him to bring Delia back and Melissa and poor Marty . . .

*   *   *

I woke up crying. It was back to the old dream. Gary had the kids and I couldn't get to them and I knew he was going to hurt them and keep them from me. I had it over and over through the years. Less often now, but still once in a while it came to haunt my sleep.

"Morning, Mom." Joey was just coming in after walking the dog. I was glad he hadn't heard my cries. He asked me how things had been at the Center last night. And I told him about Iris and Marty, the phone call about Delia. This compassionate young man was a far cry from the sassy teenager I had had to scold on the phone just last night. He went on to quiz me about Melissa.

I described the pathetic little birthday party we had given her.

"That's really awful, Mom. Where're her parents?"

"They gave her up when she was four. She was in foster homes and then adopted. Just a big mess, Joey. Nobody's ever been good to her, so now she doesn't know how to accept it even when somebody wants to be good."

"You work hard, Mom. She's lucky to have you."

"Why thanks, Joey, and I'm lucky to have you. Have a good day, and good luck with the test. You can do it! I'm going to lie down for an hour or so till Jess gets up. I'm still kind of tired. Goodbye, honey." I kissed him on the cheek.

The next time I woke the phone was ringing. Jessie was heading toward it. It was almost nine o'clock.

"Just a minute," I heard Jessie reply. "Ma, it's Sergeant Barnes."

"Okay, I'm coming. Good morning, honey," I said as we passed in the hallway. "You better get going—it's past nine," I lied. She took forever to get ready.

70

"Good morning, Frank. Any news about Heather's killer?"

"No, not really. The pimp was picked up for questioning, but we don't think he knows anything or had anything to do with it. We're questioning the girls who knew her too. It doesn't sound good."

"What do you mean?"

"She had a reputation for some pretty kinky stuff. I guess she was high all the time, go with any trick, you know?"

I winced. "Well, that's what she thought she was worth."

"No, I guess she didn't think too highly of herself."

"What's important, Frank, is that she was just a kid and she never had it decent, she had shit all her life, she was used to it. I'm sure she was waiting for the streets to kill her."

Frank paused for a moment. Then he said, "Actually I called about somebody else."

I held my breath, waiting for him to go on.

"I saw Beth out working last night. Have you seen her lately?"

"Oh, off and on," I said. "She doesn't always work the Times Square area. To tell you the truth, I'm relieved when she doesn't. I get so damn frustrated when I see her and can't speak to her. I hate having to watch her work, Frank!"

"I know, Trudee," he said sympathetically. "I told her to go see you. She was working over on Lexington in the Twenties. Maybe she'll come in."

"I appreciate it, Frank. What did she say?"

"Oh, the same, that she'd been meaning to call you or stop by. We both know her pimp watches her pretty closely."

There's an understatement, I thought. "The only way she can come to see me, Frank, is if she leaves him. She usually doesn't do that unless she gets a bad beating."

"I know how frustrating it is, Trudee, believe me. Please keep in touch and keep your ears open."

"You know I will, Frank. But please find Heather's killer before he gets another one." Beth, for example, I was thinking, but I didn't dare say it.

"I'd like nothing better, Trudee. Homicide's got it now."

Now it was Beth to worry about. It really was endless. Just the other day I had climbed the steps out of the subway station and stood breathing the fresher air for a minute, glad to be out from below. I hadn't taken two steps when I saw Beth up the street just a few feet away. She was standing in front of the transient hotel on the corner. Our eyes met for a few seconds. I wanted so much to talk to her. But her eyes warned me not to even acknowledge her presence. Her pimp was undoubtedly in the bar across the street, watching everything she did. Before I turned to cross, I gave her a small sad smile. I walked across the street and continued uptown. I wanted to turn and look back, but I knew I mustn't. Every man I passed on the street seemed to be a customer hurrying into Beth's young arms, and I hated them all.

Beth used to tell me she grew up in a dark place. She said the room where she slept with Tommy, Crystal, Baby, and her mom had brown walls. Out in the hallway, a single lightbulb swung, creating shadows that scared the girl when she was small.

Her mother worked in the nursing home on Lexington Avenue and 138th Street, near their tenement in Harlem. But there was never enough of anything.

72

It was her uncle who provided the occasional breaks from poverty for them. Beth adored him. On Christmas he always remembered his sister's children with fruit baskets and presents.

Uncle Ready also introduced Beth to the so-called finer things in life when she was thirteen. He raped her first and then "turned her out"—put her to work as a prostitute. When I met her I guess she hated him more than anything or anyone on earth. She'd run away from this "uncle" after a few weeks, taking her evenings' earnings with her. She decided to get a real job and make it on her own.

"Why didn't you ask your mother for help, honey?" I asked Beth.

"She loved him," Beth answered. "I didn't want her to know what he really was. I did tell her finally, two years later, but only because then I was afraid he'd do the same thing to my sister Crystal."

"What happened then?"

"My mom almost had a breakdown, and my uncle put Crystal out anyway. I think my mom thought it was my fault."

Two days after Beth ran away she was broke. She could no longer pay the twenty dollars a night for her cheap, smelly room. Nobody would hire her. They didn't believe her when she said she was eighteen. She hung out at the Port Authority bus station for a few days, living on doughnuts and sodas. Then she didn't eat for two days. On the third day she was standing outside a restaurant on 43rd and Eighth, looking at the food and crying. That was when a tall, well-dressed black man asked her if he could be of assistance to her.

When I met her, she had been working for him for two and a half years, on and off. She was sixteen and had been busted for prostitution exactly twenty-one times and beaten by her pimp fourteen times—one broken arm. Finally, her pimp was seriously wounded in a knife fight with another pimp. He was in the hospital for a month before Beth decided to leave him. She thought she wanted out of "the life." Maybe she was just lonely; she hadn't been alone since she met him. She heard about this place near Times Square from some of the other girls. She would go there just to talk, maybe.

When I first met with Beth at the Center, she sat with her arms folded. I would notice in time that she always did that, as if she were still protecting her body from violation and abuse. She told me her story matter-of-factly, without emotion. It was exactly what was in the file.

"Do you miss him?" I asked about her pimp.

"I don't know. Used to him, I guess."

"How about when he beats you?"

I thought I saw her jaw clench a little, but she regained composure immediately.

"I just block it out. I don't feel it much."

She stayed four days and then disappeared. I thought her pimp might be out of the hospital by now. I put her file away and sighed for the girl I might never see again.

Two days later she was back.

"Hi, sweetheart," I greeted her, "where did you go?"

"Home," she answered despondently.

"What happened, Beth?"

"My mother threw me out. She said I had caused all the troubles in our family."

"Oh, honey," I said as she moved into my arms.

Now the feelings came. Her body shook as she sobbed out the pain of the last three years. I closed the door and held her close. If she really let go, maybe she

74

could make it. Unless the bitterness and pain got out, she didn't have a chance. I knew from my experience with Heather that it does no good to hold it in.

It was the closest she'd ever allowed me to come. Usually she'd argue that I couldn't know, couldn't understand what her life was like.

"I know it's been different from mine in many ways, Beth" I told her, "but there are things that we've both experienced, too."

"Did you ever feel hungry, Miss White Counselor?" she challenged me, "or did your 'uncle' put *you* on the streets?"

"Beth . . ." I began.

"Shit, lady, you don't know nothin' about my life!"

"Okay, okay, but turning tricks is universal. The same damn feelings, the same damn men, Beth. It hurts the same way."

"It's all I know now," she said quietly.

I wondered then if I could ever help her. I felt small and helpless in the face of her long-term pain.

She stayed for another week and left again. This time I was pretty certain she went back to her pimp. Looking for a replacement for the family who threw her away. And sure enough, she was out on the streets once more.

"Ma, can you get me a towel?" Jessie called.

Why do children always go into the bathroom without checking for toilet paper or towels? I reached into the linen closet and got one of the two clean towels left.

If I hurried, I could do a load of laundry before I went down to see Melissa.

I sat in the laundry room thinking about what I could get for Melissa today. A new life isn't a bad idea, I thought as I folded the towels.

"You almost ready, Jess?" I called out a few minutes later upstairs.

Jessie and I started down the small hill to the subway station. I wanted people to see us and say, "Oh, there go a nice mother and daughter!" I didn't know what that meant exactly. I loved being a mother, *most* of the time. There were days when, after working with kids all day and coming home to hear Joe and Jess arguing, I wanted to be on an island where no one under twenty-five was admitted. Today I felt good, whole, out with my lovely daughter. I didn't feel I lived through my kids because I was doing what I wanted and accomplishing something. But I knew that mothering and nurturing were a big part of my life.

Jess kissed me goodbye and got off at 59th. I continued downtown to the hospital.

I couldn't get a pass, Melissa already had two guests. Not the pimp, I thought, panicking. I ran to the social worker's office and waited anxiously while she phoned the nurses' station in Pediatrics to find out who was visiting Melissa. It was not her pimp. Reassured, I went out again and bought a pad and two pencils for her. When I returned to the hospital, I slipped by the guard and went upstairs without a pass. Friar Bill and Annie sat by Melissa's bed. I was enormously relieved. I crossed the room and kissed Melissa's cheek. She gave me her shy-glad smile that always turned my heart to jelly.

"Hi," she said.

"You look pretty good, kid. How do you feel?"

"Better, but not terrific."

I handed her the pad and pencils. I noticed fresh flowers and two cards on her bed table. I smiled at Annie.

She stood up. "I have to get back to work." She kissed Melissa. "Get well, okay?"

"Thanks for coming and for the flowers and card," Melissa said shyly.

I walked Annie to the elevator. "When will she get out?" she asked.

"I don't know for sure, I hope to talk with her doctor today."

"Will she come back to the Center?"

"Where else? Thanks a lot, Annie. It was nice of you."

"I like her," she said as the elevator door closed.

". . . and I used to draw a lot when I was still in school," Melissa was saying to Friar Bill. "Art was my favorite class. I like to draw animals, especially babies. Oh, Trudee, thanks, it's perfect!" she said pointing to the pad on her lap.

She sat pale and small against the white hospital sheets, wearing the yellow nightgown I'd brought her yesterday.

"It looks nice, right? And it fits perfect," she said, her hand touching the frills on the little cap sleeves.

A nurse came in the room with a thermometer and blood-pressure unit. "Well, you sure have company today, and look at your beautiful flowers," she said warmly.

Melissa was glowing.

"I've got to get going," Friar Bill said. "I'm working the three-o'clock shift. Haf a goot afternoon visit mit der kinder here," he teased in his Minnesota Swedish accent.

"Ya vell you too, goot Brudder," I answered joining the silliness. We were Scandinavians from Minnesota and often did this little routine.

Melissa laughed out loud and the thermometer fell out of her mouth. The nurse frowned.

"C'mon," I said, "I'll walk you out so the nurse can do her job."

"Goodbye, Melissa. I'll come and see you Saturday or Sunday afternoon," he said taking her hand.

"Hank you hor coming," she managed without losing the thermometer again.

Out in the corridor, I said, "I'm sure you and Annie really made her feel good. Oh, look at the baby!" I exclaimed, seeing a newborn through a window in one of the other Pediatrics rooms. "It's so small!"

A nurse placed the perfect infant into a crib and came out of the room.

"Is it sick? It's so tiny," I said.

"No," she said. "She's been abandoned, she's just here for a complete check. She'll probably go to the foundling home or temporary foster care tomorrow. She seems healthy enough," the nurse said, shaking her head.

Bill and I exchanged looks—such softies both of us—ready to cry. He shook his head sadly.

"Oh, Bill, pray for this one, pray that she gets a good home."

"I already am," he answered softly.

I went back to the room and pulled a chair close to Melissa's bed. "Well, you've had a busy day. Do you really feel better?"

"It doesn't hurt so much down there any more."

"Good, then the antibiotics are doing their job. Have you met the social worker?"

"Yeah."

"She seems okay," I said encouragingly.

"I guess so." She'd dealt with too many, she wasn't exactly enthusiastic.

"We're both wondering if you'd see a psychiatrist."

"I'm not crazy!" she said angrily, sitting forward.

"I'm not suggesting you are, honey. We would like to get a psych to recommend you for placement in New York City. It would help if we had one on our side."

"Fuck. I've seen about a hundred psychiatrists. They ask you some weird shit. I think they're bugged."

I laughed. "I know, babe, some of them certainly act like it. It's important for our case, though. Do you understand?"

"I guess so." She sighed, sinking back against the pillow.

"Let me fluff you up," I said, arranging her pillows. She held herself up on two thin bare arms. "There, how's that?"

"Fine, Trudee." She bit her lip. "Did anybody ever . . . I mean, when you were little, did . . . anybody ever . . . mess with you?" She wrinkled her forehead.

I was catapulted back to a farm in North Dakota, where four-year-old Trudee saw the hired man running toward the farmhouse.

"Mrs. Able! Mrs. Able! It's Joe! He fell in the haymow. I think he's had a heart attack!"

"Mama, Mama, what's a heart tack?" I begged, frightened by the white look on her face. Moments later I was in the car with the hired man on the way to the school in town to get my brother Bo.

I rushed into the first classroom I found. "Where's my brother? My daddy is dead!" The teacher took me by the hand and we walked down the long school-smelling corridor to the seventh- and eighth-grade room. The door swung open and I could see my brother at his desk. The teacher motioned for him to come outside.

"Bo, Daddy is dead!" I said excitedly.

I felt sorry for Bo on the short drive home. He was crying, and I had made him cry. Bo never cried. I knew I must have done something very bad. Maybe it was the thing I said about Daddy.

I knew Daddy was gone because everybody kept saying it and he didn't come in to eat. At supper that night everybody was quiet and sad-looking. All the neighbors were there, even my aunt and uncle from Minot. I wanted everybody to feel better. "We'll always remember he was a good daddy," I said between mouthfuls of mashed potatoes. Everybody started crying and left the table. I'd done it again.

We moved into town sometime that year or the next. I guess the farm was too much for my mother to handle. We had over two thousand acres. I missed running through the fields. There were oceans of wheat, oats, flax, and barley: my very special playground. I had loved going out there with Mama at noon to take dinner to Daddy and Bo and the hired men. We'd unwrap the tin plates from the clean white dishtowels and inside would be potatoes, and meat swimming in gravy and thick slices of homemade bread.

When I started first grade, my world felt good. For a couple of years I enjoyed living in town, where you could get to the store with your nickel in a minute. You could even have dinner in Salter's Restaurant if you had sixty cents. The town kids would get together on Saturdays and put on carnivals with wagon-wheel rides and fish ponds. Sometimes later, we would climb into the backseat of an old Packard with gray velvety seats that belonged to someone's parents, and there in the dark garage five or six of us would play doctor. I had never seen intercourse except with animals and hadn't really connected that to human beings yet. But some of the kids knew more than I did, and we attempted intercourse. Once Danny Lindstrom got so excited he peed on Sara Tanner, and we thought she was going to have a baby. We told our mothers and we all got whippings.

One night my brother caught me behind the gazebo in the park with a boy, both of us with our pants down, rubbing furiously. He blackmailed me, taking my week's allowance, and never told.

When I stayed overnight with my best friend Kathy in second grade, she taught me a game called "wild woman." Each person took one pillow, straddled it, and rocked like crazy. And so I began to be sexually aware, even as an eight-year-old.

When my mother started dating a traveling car salesman, my world began to seem less than perfect. I didn't like this man. Gene made me very uncomfortable. When Mama talked about marrying him I got upset. I didn't want a new daddy! I had a daddy somewhere, didn't I? Why did he leave me? I wanted him back now. I must have been a very bad girl, I thought, for my daddy to leave me for good. But I was sorry now and I would be good. I wouldn't go in back of the old Packard any more or behind the gazebo. I knew that was bad. Maybe that was why Daddy left, because I was nasty. My daddy was tall and handsome, even at seventy-six, when he died. The car salesman was short and fat and had a red face. Oh, I wanted my own daddy!

My mother was only forty-two, and she was lonely in a town of married people. She must have welcomed the chance to leave with the thirty-six-year-old car salesman.

We moved to a dairy farm in Wisconsin and I started third grade. I was still nasty because I played those games with my boy cousins whenever we got a chance. I also began consciously masturbating. I didn't know what it was, except I knew I should never get caught. By the time I was eleven, I had become embarrassed about touching my changing body.

I was alone on a big farm, three miles from the closest playmate. Sometimes I would ride my bicycle all that way to have a companion for the afternoon, but mostly I played alone. I spent hundreds of hours in the playhouse deep in the woods of the pasture with my new dog Tippy. I read books and played out real scenes with Tippy as my leading man. No dolls for me. I had a constant stream of baby kittens, chicks, and calves. A large haymow to romp in and acres of cornfields for hide and seek. An idyllic farm life? No, I was miserable. I wanted friends. I hated country life and farming. When we got a TV I ached to go to the places I saw, to live in a city with lots of people. My stepfather drank and he and Mama fought a lot about that. My oldest brother, Chris, got married and moved away. And Bo, at seventeen, quit school, went into the service, and soon after got married, too.

With Bo gone, my world was empty. I idolized my brother. Even though he used to treat me pretty rough, at least he was there. I could hardly contain the excitement I felt when he came home on leave. He was so handsome in his Army uniform. I was even taken with his pretty new wife wearing her first maternity smocks.

One day Bo, his new wife, Mama, and I came home at milking time and found the sterilized milking machines overturned in the barn. The cows stood crying in their stalls, their bags full of milk.

Bo ran to the house after my stepfather. Covered with cowshit, Gene lay on Mama's clean white bedspread. He'd taken off all his clothes except a T-shirt and left them in a pile on the floor. As Bo jumped toward him, Mama shoved me out of the room. I watched them shoving each other in the hallway and fighting their way toward the kitchen. Mama opened the basement door and pushed me inside. But not before I saw my stepfather with blood dripping from his face, down his shirt, and onto his penis. It was a huge hairy bloody monster. I would have nightmares about it for years.

Things got better for me when the old couple moved in next door. It wasn't like having kids live nearby, but in some ways it was even better. I had never known grandparents and now I had a grandmother and grandfather of my own in the persons of Hannah and Hank Olson. They doted on me. I spent hours at their house. Hank made rings out of dimes for me and a cupboard for a doll house and Hannah baked all my special cookies and listened patiently to my fantasies of being an actress or at least a singer-dancer, even though she was a strict Baptist. In fact, they were so horrified to learn that, at eleven and a half, I wasn't even baptized that they hauled me over to the Baptist church and signed me up for Bible Camp to get "saved."

In the evenings at their house, Hank and Hannah

would drag out the big old homemade game board. Hank and I would play one of the dozens of interesting games while Hannah baked something delicious for me. As I later discovered, they were brother and sister. They had no grandchildren, which was fine with me. I didn't want to share them with anyone.

One day when I rode over to see them I called from my bike in the yard into the house for Hannah. Hank came out, and his face lit up with pleasure at seeing me. "Hannah's gone to town to do some work at the church," he said, coming over to me. He put his hands up under my little summer top and touched my barely visible bud breasts. "What's this?" he said, patting them and looking right into my face.

I tore out of there, riding home as fast as possible, and went into my house hysterically crying. It took a while before Mama got the story straight. All of a sudden, I felt like I had done something wrong, because she stayed very quiet.

"Don't worry, I'll take care of it, toots," she finally said. She got up and went outside and got in the car. She was back in a few moments. "Don't go over there unless Hannah is home, Trudee, okay?"

"I'll never go over there again," I screamed, escaping to my room and slamming the door. It was my fault, I was the one who made that old man get dirty. After all, he hadn't been that way before I got breasts, and I grew the breasts.

The incident was never mentioned in my house again. When I saw Hank in town I would cross the street to avoid him. I can still see him standing beside his old green car at the other end of the street watching me.

A few years later, Mama and my stepfather got a divorce, and once again we were selling the farm and moving to town. From watching "Father Knows Best" I found out how abnormal my life was. Those people never drank or fought or went to the toilet or played with little girls. There were no stepparents.

I grew up feeling self-conscious at all times. I was always sure that I had a run in my nylons or my slip was showing. It didn't matter how new my dress was or how nicely my hair was done, I always felt awkward, like I didn't quite belong to the mainstream of life. I also had a lot of dreams about being caught naked in public, which convinced me that I was a real nasty type.

Maybe that's why discovering my sexual power had so much importance for me.

I remember in seventh grade wanting to be a nun. I had just learned that such women existed and I thought it was the most noble thing I had ever heard of. I was going to the Lutheran church that year because most of my friends went there. In the Christmas play, I was cast as Magdalene.

After the incident with Hank Olson my body felt dirty. I was always in conflict about it. I thought if my breasts would stop growing I could stay hidden in childhood. Yet I desperately wanted to grow up. I would stand naked in front of the mirror trying to decide which I was, an adult or a child. But of course, I had no choice in the matter, and soon my breasts were developing more quickly than I could ever have imagined. I had the biggest bust in the eighth grade.

So far all the men in my life had left me. Daddy had died, Chris was in jail, and Bo was in the Army. Even Hank was lost to me too.

Now I was very attracted to the boys at school. I wanted their attention desperately. And I noticed that since I'd gotten the breasts, I was getting a lot more of it. I figured out that they were just younger versions of Hank. It didn't seem so bad if they were my own age. I hadn't wanted that kind of attention from Hank, but if my bust made me popular with the boys at school, well, it must be my greatest asset.

I also wanted to be glamorous. So I donned the skimpy sweaters that showed off my figure.

One day I pulled on my favorite pink angora sweater and the burgundy straight skirt that I loved to wear with it. I put on a pair of pink anklets and looked for my saddle shoes. I found one under my bed.

"Ma, where's my other saddle shoe?"

"Wherever you took it off!" she called from the kitchen.

Oh great, she was a lot of help. I found it in the closet finally. I looked in the full-length mirror behind the closet door and admired myself, turning around to see all angles.

"Boy, David Henderson will *have* to talk to me today," I said to the mirror.

"You better get down the driveway, the bus'll be here in five minutes," Mama called.

I grabbed my coat and ran to the kitchen. Mama stood at the counter, her hands full of bread dough. Her apron had flour dusted all over it where she'd wiped her hands.

"You should eat something, toots."

"I'm not hungry, Mama. Bye!" I yelled, running out the door.

Carrie and I spent as much time before class as possible in the bathroom talking about David Henderson. I loved him. Carrie was the only one who knew how I felt. He hadn't been in our school very long and so far he wasn't writing notes to any other girls in class. I still had a chance. When the last bell rang Carrie and I stuffed our Natural Lipsticks in our newly acquired purses and rushed across the hall.

By ten o'clock I found a reason to walk to the back of the room past David's desk. I slid out of my seat with my broken pencil and walked down the aisle. Now take a right and two aisles over was the sacred desk that my love occupied. He looked up as I went by. Some of the other boys did too. I was glad I had worn the pink sweater. I tried to smile at David, but I'm sure the smile froze on my lips. Darn.

At last it was time for lunch. The morning had taken forever. I thought I should sharpen my pencil again just as the lunch bell rang. It didn't hurt to have a sharp pencil for the afternoon, I told myself.

I saw David looking at me again as I went by his desk. Oh, I was sure he liked me. I busied myself with the sharpener. Then I sneaked a look at David and saw him lean over and whisper to the boy next to him. I took two steps toward his desk to return to my seat when I heard him whisper, "Look at her in that tight skirt and sweater. She really looks awful." His face was wrinkled and disgusted.

I must have made some sound because the two boys turned and saw me. At least he had the decency to look embarrassed. I turned and fled to the bathroom, locked myself in the stall, and started to cry. I looked down at my pretty pink sweater and felt only loathing. I pulled at the front to loosen it. It wasn't too tight, it wasn't. Well okay, maybe David didn't like my clothes, but the older boys did. He could just go to hell. Who needed him anyway? I kept wearing my sweaters and got the attention I needed from the boys in high school. I didn't know it yet, but it was the wrong kind.

When my brother Bo went to jail the whole town found out. It was in the local papers. Now I was Bo

Able's sister. I was never just Trudee Able again. I was Bo's or Chris's sister. I must be like them, the town thought. If they're always in trouble, then the girl must be loose. So I set out to prove they were right and bought even tighter sweaters. I hated my body, yet I knew the power it gave me. It was the only power I had.

I was a friendly person, sensitive and creative. There was nowhere to channel the goodness or love I felt. I couldn't talk to Mama about the things I felt. She didn't seem to know what to do with me at all.

One time my class wrote essays about what we wanted to be, and then we all read them aloud. Everybody wanted to be farmers or salesmen or teachers. There was one stewardess. Then I read mine. I wanted to be a famous actress like Sarah Bernhardt. Everybody laughed, including the teacher.

More and more, I learned to keep everything inside or talk to my mirror. I put on plays for a couple of girlfriends in their garage, but they were sworn to secrecy.

I stopped joining the talent show at school each year and stopped begging my mother for dance and singing lessons. I quit choir and stopped playing saxophone in the school band. Soon even the plays stopped. I was too old for a kid's dreams. I was fourteen, and I had a rep. All the boys wanted to take me home from basketball games. Never *to* the games, just home. I already knew how a whore felt.

I got a bra and my period that same year. I knew people talked about my divorced mother, but they also respected her. She worked hard, kept a decent house, and belonged to the homemakers club. She was so sweet and friendly that if anybody disapproved of her she wouldn't have known. I knew, though. How could

I have been born into this imperfect family?

Which was becoming more imperfect by the minute. Even though they were divorced, my stepfather, Gene, was still hanging around, trying to woo Mama back. Between his trips to our house looking for Mama, he hung around the bar, so he was pretty drunk most of the time. One day he was waiting for her when she drove home from work with her new boyfriend in the car. The two men got into a horrible, bloody fight in the backyard.

For all I hated my stepfather, I realized that I hated this new boyfriend even more. "Stop it, you're killing him!" I shouted at the big, ugly slob who was kicking Gene's head as he lay bleeding on the grass. "Stop it! I hate you! I hate you! I'm going to call the police!" I ran toward the house.

"No, Trudee, don't. I'll stop him," Mama yelled.

"To hell with you," I yelled back. "You started it."

I called the town sheriff, ran back outside where the neighbors were beginning to gather, and my seventeen-year-old neighbor grabbed my arm and led me sobbing to her car. We rode around for a while, and she took me for some supper. When she brought me home later, my mother wasn't there. We found several neighbors clustered in her yard.

"Where's my ma?" I asked.

They looked at each other. I noticed one of the neighbors had been crying. "She doesn't know," another said.

"What is it? Where's my mother?" I said, my voice rising.

It seems that when the sheriff came, he and my mother had managed to get my stepfather up out of the yard and into the kitchen to feed him some black coffee. The sheriff told Gene he was going to lock him up for the night for his own safety because he didn't want him driving home in that shape. Gene bolted out of the house, jumped into his car, and went careening out of the driveway. The sheriff chased him to stop him. On a treacherous corner called Trap Rock, because of the steep rock that lined the south side of the highway, my stepfather smashed himself and his car to bits.

Mama was out dancing with her boyfriend. When they came home I screamed and accused them of murdering Gene. I cried over and over, "He's going to kill Bo too! He's going to kill Bo too!"

I always worried about poor Bo. He seemed to get into all kinds of trouble, but I did love him so. Now I was scared that this man was going to do something to take Bo away from me too.

Sure enough, soon after the dreadful incident with Gene, Bo escaped from prison and made his way back home. Running through the swamps with dogs chasing him, crossing the country through fields and ditches, he somehow managed to get all the way to our house. I wasn't there, but I heard Mama tell her boyfriend what he looked like—skinny and gaunt and dirty and sick. Mama turned him in. She said she couldn't stand to see him like that. The whole town knew.

School started just after that, and it was an exciting time in spite of the horrors of my home life. I was really entering high school now, almost an adult. I could hardly wait.

But the first day of school some of the older boys called out to me, "Hey, jailbird."

I didn't hang my head or do anything else to look ashamed. I just mumbled, "Fuckers," and kept going. But the next day I wore a tighter sweater. I knew I had the biggest bust in my class if not in the whole school.

90

Then "jailbird" wasn't all they called me. They started referring to me as "slut" and "whore," and they talked in their locker-room showers about how they'd had me. The story was that my bust was big because I let all the boys play with it. The fact was that nobody had ever touched me. Except for Hank Olson.

Melissa sat quietly through my story of Hank Olson and my trust betrayed, my tale of growing up in a town of six hundred with a pair of big tits. Neither of us said a word for a few minutes after I'd finished talking. I reached out to take her hand and looked at her pitifully chewed-off fingernails. "I used to do that too," I said softly.

"Why did he do it?" she said suddenly. "Why did my adopted father do that stuff to me? He was supposed to be my father! What made him like that with me?"

"Oh honey, I'm not sure." She had asked her question so piteously. "Often people who abuse children sexually *and* physically were abused themselves when they were little," I said. I tried to explain it all to her as best I could. I told her that sometimes adults who are disappointed, unfulfilled by adult sex seem to think they can, through children, return to their adolescence. That was a period when sex was still new and unspoiled, so their sexual interaction with kids makes them feel excited again. We just don't know enough about incest and child molesting yet. What I didn't tell her were my fears about how long it would take to learn enough to make a difference in the lives of kids like her. But I did assure her that work had begun and that she was not alone.

"It happens a lot, Melissa—more than people will admit yet." I looked into her eyes to see if she understood. Pain stared out at me. "Honey, almost as

91

bad as the experience itself is carrying it around inside of you. It wasn't you, Melissa, it was him, *his* problem. You just happened to be in the wrong place at the wrong time."

She didn't say anything. I honored the silence, letting my words to her sink in. Finally she looked up at me. "You know, when I told them at school—what he did—they didn't believe me. At least they didn't do anything. Then it happened to my girlfriend and they finally listened."

"It really hurts not to be believed," I agreed. "Sometimes I think that's as destructive as anything that happened."

"I felt like it was my fault, or like I was dirty for saying it."

"Would you like to tell me about it?" I asked gently. "We talked about it some when you were at the Center. You were pretty high that night, do you remember?"

Melissa nodded. "I knew I told you," she said. "I always wonder what people think about me, so I haven't told many people. I haven't talked about it much for a long time now." She shifted in the bed, pulling the covers up higher as if to protect herself. "After I accused Mr. James," she said, taking a deep breath, "they gave me up, like I had done something bad. I felt like I was bad, like I didn't deserve a nice family, 'cause I wasn't nice." She turned her head away, toward the wall.

"I think you're awfully nice," I said, taking her face in my hands and turning it toward me. My eyes told her I meant it, but could she ever believe it?

"Mr. James made me do things." She hesitated.

I encouraged her. "Where was Mrs. James, Melissa?"

"At the store or visiting friends. I used to beg her to take me with her. But she'd tell me to stay home and be

92

good," Melissa said bitterly. "Then *he* would say, 'That's all right, I don't mind taking care of her.' It made my skin crawl when he said that. I used to lock myself in the bathroom, but he always got me out." She stared up at the ceiling.

"How did he get you out?" I asked, stroking her arm.

"First he'd tell me he wouldn't hurt me. Then he'd say if I didn't come out he'd tell her. She was always the one who did the hitting. Next he'd say if I didn't come out right away he'd call the police and they'd lock me in a dark place with rats and snakes!" Her voice broke into a plaintive wail. The tears slid down her cheeks. "That got me every time," she cried, clenching her teeth. I stroked and squeezed her arm. "Then when I came out he'd grab me and say, 'Got ya.' I was so afraid of snakes I used to have nightmares about them!" She sobbed and the shoulders under her new yellow gown shook.

"Oh honey, I'm sorry," I said, sitting on the bed and taking her in my arms. She pulled away for just a second, then let go completely in my arms, clinging to me, sobbing. "I'm so sorry," I repeated, rocking her gently. "That would damn sure have got me out of the bathroom when I was little." I smoothed her hair off her face and wiped her tears when the sobs subsided.

When she spoke again her voice was calm and cold. "He'd take me upstairs then, to their bed. Then he'd play-spank me and say—he had—to—kiss it to make it better." She shuddered in my arms. I held on tight. "Then he'd turn me over and . . . I've never talked about it like this before. I hate him!"

"Let it go if you can, honey, and we'll get through this," I pleaded. I wanted her to get past the experience.

"He made me touch his—and tried to put it in me!

He hurt me and I screamed at him, 'Please stop it!'"
She pulled the covers up over her mouth. "He pushed
my head down and pushed my mouth and face on—
him!" She moaned through the sheet. "Oh God," she
wailed turning to the wall, "I hate him so much—I hate
both of them!"

She wept softly. I kissed the back of her head and
rubbed her arm. "How often, Melissa?"

"About five or six times till she caught us," she said
sniffling.

"That must have been an awful scene for you," I
said. "But, honey, she caught him, not you."

"She beat me and called me names. She said I was a
nasty girl and that I'd go to hell. She called me a little
whore! I mean I was eight and a half! I didn't know
what it was, but I knew it was bad. She locked me in
my room and I could hear them fighting. I cried all
night till I fell asleep." Her eyes were glazed from the
pain and memory.

I tried to calm her down some more. "Melissa, I
know it was terrible for you, but it wasn't anything you
caused."

She just kept going, as if now that she had begun to
let it pour out there was no stopping it. "It didn't
happen again for a few months," Melissa told me. "She
was watching him all the time at first. Then—it started
all over again. Finally I told a teacher at school, and she
seemed, uh, embarrassed you know? Nothing happened, nothing changed. And I had been so scared to
tell her. I thought God would come out of heaven and
strike me dead, and then nothing even happened."

Melissa told me that she had been afraid to tell
anybody else because she felt so dirty. She used to
sneak away if Mrs. James went someplace and hide
somewhere till she got back. After a similar incident

happened to a little friend of hers who told her story at school, a teacher or nurse took Melissa to a small office, asked her all sorts of questions, and then took her to a doctor.

"It was awful!" she said. "They took me to a foster home that night, the nurse and a lady from the welfare."

She turned and snuggled against me for comfort. I held tight to her. Neither of us spoke for a while. I stroked her hair, hardly trusting myself to say anything. I could have killed for her then: my maternal instincts were as strong as they'd ever been. I saw it all in my mind: a frightened, unwanted kid cowering in the corner of the bathroom; afterward her face burning shame into the bedspread as that sick old bastard "made it better"; then the terrifying snake dreams, which the "experts" probably pronounced phallic. A little girl, plagued by negative sexuality twenty-four hours a day.

I kissed her forehead. "Melissa—"

"Hmmm?" she responded, her voice barely audible.

"I believe you—I know that this ugliness happened to you."

"I know you do."

I held her at arm's length and looked into her eyes, smoothing her hair away from her tear-stained face. "I know you're never going to forget it, honey, but try to let it go. It's *his* problem, sweetheart, *not yours*. Let it be his. Just as it happened to your girlfriend and to me, it happens to any little girl who comes along when an adult has a sickness like that."

"I guess you're right. I never really thought about it like that. . . . Trudee—I feel bad, but good, you know? I'm glad I told you. I could never really talk about it like this before."

I told Melissa that I knew what that felt like, too. There was never anyone I could talk to at home. The first time I ran away was the summer Mama was going with the bee man. I hated him as much as I had the one who was responsible for Gene's death. This one kept bees and had warts on his face. I didn't like either.

Bo was home from prison again and I was fourteen, almost fifteen. By now any boy who thought he was a real man had said I'd gone down. I kept trying to find boyfriends from other towns who wouldn't know my reputation.

Bo went to live in Minneapolis with his second wife and baby. When he came up one weekend at the beginning of the summer, I told him Mama was out at the bee man's. He went out to see her and found her in bed with her boyfriend. He charged back to our house and told me about it. Now my Mama was in her fifties and certainly had a right to sleep with whomever she wanted, but we, her children, didn't quite see it that way. Maybe it was because we hated the bee man so much. I don't know.

I took off for Minneapolis. First I stayed with Bo, then with a girl I met. I got a job in a factory by lying about my age—I said I was sixteen and pretended I was all grown up. I soon discovered that it wasn't so much fun paying the rent and fighting off the guys I dated after all. I met a boy named Raymond Silvera who was so handsome I thought I'd die. He was Mexican and I'd never seen the likes of him. All we had at home were Swedes and Norwegians. I wanted to go out with him, but I was terrified.

Mama finally came and got me with her new fiancé. I didn't like him either, but I thought he was better than the bee man—but then anybody was. We would be moving to another town a few miles away. I hated leaving my friend Carrie and protested vehemently to no avail. Carrie was vivacious and her bright energy helped me some to forget my problems. She was from a normal home with wonderful parents and she had offered to share them with me whenever I needed it. Maybe this town hadn't been good to me, but Carrie was here—and I was afraid of what a new town would do to me. Also, we were going back to the cowshit life that I despised. I was used to being a townie by now and didn't want any part of the farm.

There was only one thing that saved me. Maggie lived in the new town. We had been good friends from third to fifth grade, when her family moved. At least I'd found her again. Maggie was soft and sweet. I felt more calm when I was with her. She was from a bad home with an abusive stepfather. She was someone I could protect and stand up for.

I looked at Melissa in her hospital bed. Despite all my problems, I had clearly had a better childhood than so many others. I realized how easily I might have led a life like Melissa's—or Heather's—had I landed in the city.

Melissa was doodling on her drawing pad as I spoke. "What are you drawing, honey?"

"Oh, nothing. It's just a sort of map," she said, turning it so I couldn't see.

"C'mon, sweetheart, you know I'd love to see your work. Didn't I bring you the pad and pencils?"

She put it in front of me, but I couldn't make out what it was.

"It's a place where I used to work," she said softly.

This was a new one on me. "What did you do there?" I asked.

"Danced."

"Was this place up near the Center?" It was beginning to dawn on me.

Melissa looked down and nodded.

"A peep show?"

"Uh huh."

What she had drawn was indeed a little map of the inside of the peep show. Now I watched as her small hand drew in the stage and the booths around it where the men stood. This clearly went back to a time when Melissa had first come to the Center, a time when I knew she had been taking a lot of drugs, Tuinals, acid, angel dust, ups—anything to disguise how she was feeling inside. At the ripe old age of thirteen, she had already tried the streets for a while and now thought maybe a peep show would be better. And it had seemed so simple. A girl she'd met on the street had volunteered to meet her at a bookstore on Seventh Avenue and introduce her to her contact, Lefty.

When Melissa got there the other girl was nowhere in sight, but she went right in and asked, "Is there a Lefty works here?"

"Who wants to know?" the unshaven man behind the counter asked. She noticed two customers ogling her from the side of the store where the racks of porn magazines stood.

"Jewel," she said. She had come prepared with a stage name.

The man behind the counter picked up a phone. "Hey, there's a chick down here name of Jewel, says she wants Lefty."

"Tell him I'm a friend of Lexington Mary," she said

anxiously. The girl had told her to mention an older transvestite Melissa knew who once explained the name: "'Cause when I was younger, honey, I used to make me some good money on Lexington Avenue downtown. I thought that street was mine, honey!"

Melissa saw the two customers begin to edge their way toward her.

"Okay, baby, hold on a minute."

She stayed close to the man behind the counter. The other two made her nervous.

A man came through a door at the back. "Hi, baby," he said. "I was beginning to think you weren't coming."

She didn't say anything, just gave him a strange little crooked smile.

He led her through a door and up a flight of stairs.

"Hey, Slim, this is— What's your name, hon?"

"Jewel."

"She might be working for us," Lefty said to a man in the change booth.

They passed a string of doors that seemed to go in a semicircle.

"That's where the guys go in. Follow me." They entered a small office. "The girls' dressing room is on the other side of this. You can work from nine in the morning till six, or you can work from three till midnight. You do an hour on and a half hour off. Those booths in the back that we passed, you dance in there privately for the men, but there's a glass that separates you from the guys so they can't touch you. There's a phone in there that they can talk to you on. The stage is in the center of the regular booths. The guy puts a quarter in and the plate lifts for two minutes. He has to put another quarter in for another two minutes. He has to put in a dollar's worth of quarters in the private booths. Any tips you get are your own. You'll get seventy-five dollars a shift. Any deals you make for tricking, you do when you leave."

"When do you want me to start?"

"You got a costume?"

"No."

"Let's go buy you some stuff so you can start right now. I'm short girls." An hour later she was at work. She danced over to a booth on the side when she saw a man gesture to her. The stage was placed so he could reach only her breasts. He gave her two dollars and played with her with one hand for a few seconds. Then she felt his body shaking and heard him groan.

The clean-up man came around every few hours and threw buckets of water and Lysol on the floor to keep the stench down. But nothing could.

The next guy that gestured to her asked to see her in a private booth. She signaled to the head girl and went toward the back.

The guy opened the door and picked up the phone. "Hi, little baby," he breathed into it.

"Hi," she said woodenly.

"You're such a baby, so pretty with such smooth young skin," he said, unzipping his fly with his other hand.

"You want me to dance?" she asked.

"Oh yes, but stay on the phone, I have things to tell you, little one."

She held on to the phone and gyrated her hips slowly while the man spewed forth his filth both on the phone and on the floor. Melissa wished for him to have a heart attack. She thought she'd enjoy seeing that.

Next, it was her turn to lie on the rotating platform in the middle of the stage. One at a time, each girl had to put in some time lying there and spreading her legs.

Melissa told me she felt cold, totally numb, as she methodically went through the motions.

Melissa was much younger than the other girls, and they weren't very friendly at first. She kept a low profile and tried to stay out of their way, but they complained that she was stealing their customers. Lefty didn't tolerate too much shit from them, though. He knew Melissa was making him money.

She quit the peep show after a few weeks. It was just too much for her: the men, the smell, the things she had to say—"that goddamn obscene phone." She never even saved any money. She had to buy twice as many drugs for her head.

I thought I'd burst with feeling for her. "Oh, honey, I'm so glad you're able to tell me all this. Whenever you want to talk about hurtful things I'll be around, okay?" We sat still for some more minutes. Why had no one ever opened these floodgates before? I wondered.

"Hey, would you like a soda or something cold to drink?" I said, sitting up and straightening her covers.

"A chocolate malt?" she asked with a tiny smile.

"You got it, be right back." I took my purse and started for the door then turned and looked at her little shape huddled there on the bed. I smiled a smile that told her we'd gotten through something important, together.

Sitting in the coffee shop waiting for our order, I felt drained, spent, from the session with Melissa. Her eyes, the pain registered there had penetrated my depths. So childlike, yet so old, those eyes. It was true that Melissa's experience was not unique. From talking to dozens of other girls in prostitution, I'd found usually they had been sexually molested as children.

Melissa lay curled up, fast asleep, when I returned. I tiptoed over and kissed her cheek. Her eyes fluttered. "I'll see you tomorrow, honey," I whispered. "Rest now."

"Mmmmm," she managed as her eyes closed again. I pulled the covers gently around her and retrieved the sketch pad and pencil from the floor.

A nurse put the malt in the fridge for later and told me that Melissa's doctor was on the floor somewhere. "If you'd like to wait in the lounge for a few moments, I'll try to locate him."

"Thank you." I sank gratefully into a chair in the lounge and reached for a cigarette. I sat thinking about changing Melissa's life. What kind of a chance did I have? So much, so damn much had happened to show her it was worthless, her life.

"Ms. Peterson?"

I looked up at the young resident. "Hello, Doctor, how's Melissa doing?"

"Very well, the antibiotics are doing the work. She should be ready to go home Monday."

Home.

"Will she be returning to the Center?" he asked.

"Well, she certainly can. I guess she probably will. The only other options are Connecticut or the streets. She won't be well enough to run the streets for now anyway," I said sighing.

"She speaks very highly of you. It seems you've been able to form some sort of relationship with her."

"I care a lot about her. I just don't really know how

much I can do. Our facility isn't long-term. If I could spend the next couple of years with her, really get close, maybe, then maybe I could convince her she's not a piece of shit." I shook my head. I didn't feel as positive as I had led Melissa to believe. Was it unfair to give her hope? I felt guilty and uncomfortable with my feelings.

A few minutes later I told the social worker that Melissa would see the psychiatrist.

"Good," she said. "I spoke to her social worker in Connecticut. They certainly have no objections to her staying. They'll fund her in any group home here that will take her."

"Really?" I said, reaching for something to lift my spirits, "That's great!"

"Well, we still have to get someone to agree. Do you have any ideas?"

"Let me work on it. She can stay at the Center until we come up with something. What good news. Now if we can just hold on to her—she's pretty stubborn when she's feeling well," I said, laughing. "When will the psychiatrist see her?"

"Probably tomorrow morning."

"Okay, I'll see you tomorrow afternoon, then," I said, standing up.

I was tempted to go back upstairs and wake Melissa to tell her the good news. Instead, I pushed open the large glass doors and propelled myself forward into the bright March sunshine. My burdens seemed to lift as I walked up Seventh Avenue, counting my blessings. Melissa had shared a lot with me today. Maybe it *was* an important breakthrough for us. Maybe if she stayed in New York I could really work with her intensely. And maybe she really wouldn't have to end up like Heather or become a burned-out doper at sixteen. I climbed into the subway car, all the maybes in my mind taking me uptown, giving bare notice to the underground filth.

I was truly elated that I had made a breakthrough with Melissa. It was so important for all the past to come out before we could begin to work toward a decent future. That was more or less the way I had had to do it.

Now I realized that in opening Melissa's floodgates I seemed to have opened some of my own again too. I went back to those days just after we moved to the town where Maggie lived.

For the next two years I floated through school and home not knowing who I was or why I had been born. The only thing that sustained me was my close relationship with Maggie. I hated my new stepfather, and he wasn't really too keen on me either. Our house was a potential war zone at all times. My grades fell and I cut school as often as I could.

When Mama told me that Bo was being sent to jail again I took an overdose of some sleeping pills I found in the medicine cabinet and they had to take me to the hospital. The whole school thought I had had to go in for an abortion.

One weekend two months before graduation Maggie and her mother took me shopping in Minneapolis. I never went home. I managed to find Raymond Silvera, and this time I felt brave enough to go out with him, especially since he was just about the only person I knew there.

Raymond took me to a party. As soon as we got there he gave me a Pepsi and put two pep pills in it. After a while I started feeling sort of tense and nervous. I told him I felt strange. Things seemed distorted and I stayed close to him. Then we were in the bedroom but I could hear the people outside. Raymond was on top of me pulling at my clothes and telling me not to be afraid, it wouldn't hurt. I felt scared but unable to get out of the situation. There were other people in the apartment. Friends of his that I didn't know.

"I'm a virgin," I mumbled as he removed my panties.

"Don't worry, it will be okay. Don't be afraid."

He jabbed inexpertly at me between my legs. I wiggled my hips this way and that trying to move away from him.

"Hold still, Trudee!" he demanded.

"You're going to hurt me," I whimpered.

"It won't hurt if you hold still."

A searing pain shot through me as he finally connected and plunged forward. I screamed and he put his hand over my mouth.

"Ssh," he commanded as he pumped spasmodically.

And then it was over.

This first sexual experience was the worst disillusionment I'd had yet. Sex wasn't fun, it didn't feel good, it wasn't nice at all. In fact it was a piece of shit.

Afterward Raymond Silvera, the handsome Mexican boy, rolled over. "I thought you said you were a virgin," he said contemptuously.

I cried all that next day. I thought of all the whispers in school halls and the boys who didn't take me out because I had a reputation, and the boys who took me out because I had one. The endless struggles in the dark in cars when I wouldn't give in because I believed the fairy tale that someday I would be adored and have a good life, because I had "saved myself." So much for that.

Raymond never believed me, not even when we were married a few months later because I was pregnant. By then I hated him.

My baby was the only thing good in my world. I delivered him two months after I left Raymond: our marriage had lasted just two months. I didn't care, I had Joey.

A year later I was in the same predicament, and I got married again. This time I fooled myself for a while that I was in love, he was an acceptable, nice boy from a "good" home. I couldn't have known then that it would turn out to be a nest of hypocrites; at the time, they seemed like the "right people."

Gary was a sensitive young poet, who had read lots of books and had a few years at college. He used to read me his poems. I never knew any males before Gary who wrote poems. It seemed very romantic. We'd sit curled up on the couch reading the poems, and sometimes he would cry. If we had a fight and I'd say I was leaving him he would sit on the floor beside me, put his head on my lap, and beg me not to go. I'd never seen men cry either.

When we started making love it was very different than with Raymond. Our sexual exploration had begun as a much more pleasant relationship. Gary was gentle, if intense, and I learned about foreplay. I would get very excited by the foreplay so that when we finally had intercourse I was ready. But then, although it wasn't the cold, uncaring act it had been with Raymond, when Gary was on top of me the feelings went

106

away. All the good feelings during foreplay were lost with the act of intercourse. I felt nothing then. It confused me. I knew I was supposed to feel something. What was wrong with me?

We starved like all young couples and fought and made up by making love. Maybe I wasn't getting satisfied regularly, but at least I had felt something a few times, at least I knew it was possible.

Jessie was born, and I was happy with my two perfect children. I became a bit less happy a few months later when I had to go to work and leave her and Joey with a babysitter. I missed them during the day and resented that the babysitter got to hear Joey's first words and enjoy Jessie's baby smiles that were so precious to me. They were mine, not hers. But we did need the money.

Also around this time strange things began happening with Gary. Things I couldn't understand.

"Please, Trudee," he was saying to me one night. "I won't really hurt you, just pretend, please."

"Gary, the kids."

"They're sleeping, they'll never hear us."

"But, Gary, I'm afraid."

"I told you I won't hurt you. I'll tie you up and wrap a towel around the belt, you won't hardly feel it. We'll just go through the motions of my hurting you."

"I don't understand. It doesn't do anything for me. How come you like it?"

"Just do it, please, Trudee, please. Please, Trudee. Please, Trudee, please."

Half a bottle of cheap wine later, I agreed. Afterward I sat shaking in the bathroom.

Gary was true to his word, he hadn't actually hurt me, physically, but inside I was in great pain.

It didn't stop. He begged every week the same way—

"Please, Trudee. Please, Trudee, please." I went to my doctor, who said, "Anything two people do in the bedroom behind closed doors is permissible."

I was too embarrassed to tell my doctor exactly what Gary was doing. But I thought, Wait a damn minute, something has to be wrong with this. I read *Justine* by the Marquis de Sade and any other beat-whip stuff I could get my hands on. I still didn't understand it, and I don't to this day. How could he say, "I love you," and still want to hurt me?

I finally went to a psychiatrist because I thought there might be something wrong with me. Nobody had ever told me about those things. Maybe it was me. It seemed that I was all twisted up in sexuality since I was a little girl. The psychiatrist said I was fine but he'd like to see Gary. Gary refused. I had begun to do some crazy things living with Gary. The countless scenes and all-night pleading and the horror stories he finally got me to participate in were not my dreams of love. I had to get out before my sanity was gone. I told him I was leaving.

I stood looking around the bleak little room I'd rented for the kids and myself. Here I was, twenty-one, with two children to support, alone.

"Gary," I pleaded, some months later, above the noise at the bar where he was working, "please give me some money for groceries."

I had been working two jobs and still couldn't make ends meet. In the daytime I took care of the charge accounts and books in a nightclub restaurant for almost no money and I doubled back at night to wait on tables in a bunny-type costume. The propositions from the older men began sounding better. I doubted they would ask the same things of me that Gary had.

I hardly ever saw my small ones. I took them to the

babysitter in the morning, picked them up in the afternoon, made dinner and returned them to another babysitter for my evening shift. I knew they weren't getting good care and it was eating a hole in my heart.

Gary never went to visit the kids unless he thought I'd be home and he had a chance of having sex with me at the end of the day.

"Gary, please." I had become the one who had to beg.

He pushed the cash register buttons and said, "Just a minute."

A few minutes later he motioned me to the other end of the bar where we could talk. "I haven't got any money, Trudee, and you shouldn't come here when I'm working."

"It's the only place I can get hold of you," I said angrily. "I haven't got any food in my cupboard, Gary!"

He counted out four ones and five dollars' worth of change from his tip jar. I had to go through this every time I needed money.

For nearly three years I struggled along this way, living from day to day. And then I developed kidney trouble, which was finally diagnosed as nephritis.

"I'm afraid you'll have to check into the hospital, Trudee," my doctor told me one day.

I looked up weakly from his examining table. "I can't go to the hospital, Doctor, I have no one to take care of my children."

I was in the hospital six times that year, for two or three weeks each time—once for six weeks. I asked Mama to take care of the kids, but she said she couldn't because she had a job. She had come to see me the first time I was hospitalized, and somehow she made me feel as if I was taking her away from her own life. She didn't say she resented being there and she was very kind, but there were undertones of, "Lord, why do I have to go through this?" in her actions. Maybe her own life was all she could handle. After that, I stopped calling her when I went in.

The welfare department also asked Gary's parents to help, and they said they didn't want to get involved. The kids stayed with anyone the welfare or I could find. I found out later they were neglected and abused in some of these places. It added to the rest of the guilt I seemed to be living with always at this time. If I had been a decent person I probably wouldn't have gotten nephritis, right?

When I checked out the last time I picked up the children from their current babysitter and went to the welfare office.

"You'll have to come back on Monday so we can process your case," a brisk, cold woman said.

"But I have nowhere to stay this weekend and no food! Please can't you give me emergency funds or someplace to stay?"

"I'm sorry. That's the rule."

"But," I began, as tears fell from my eyes. Four-year-old Joey looked up at me, inquisitive and scared. The worker's stony face and pursed lips told me it would do no good to beg. I shook myself and stood up. Tears dripping down my face, I started to put on the children's coats. "It's people like you who make prostitutes out of women like me!" I shouted at the room full of workers. They stared at me like I was a fungus.

"Hello, Joann?" I said into the telephone.

"Hi, Trudee, honey, what's up?" She was obviously surprised to hear from me. Joann was a "working-girl" who came to the nightclub where I worked before I became ill. She had offered to "show me the ropes" many times.

"Joann, I have no place to go and no money and no food for Joey and Jessie!" I sobbed into the phone. "I don't know what to do. I can't go home to my mother—my stepfather probably wouldn't let me in anyway, he hates me. My brother Bo is way out in California, I don't even know where to find him. I can't ask Gary for help . . ."

"Whoa, Trudee, hold on, I can hardly understand you. Where are you?"

"Around the corner from the welfare office downtown—I don't know what I'm going to do."

"Trudee, come on over and we'll talk. Please."

"Do you have customers there?"

"No." She laughed. "And if anyone calls I'll say no. Jump in a cab and get over here."

"I haven't got cab fare," I said weakly.

"Get in a cab. I'll watch for you and pay the driver."

"Thanks, Jo."

I called a cab from the drugstore and tried to explain to Joey why I couldn't buy him a Coke and potato chips. He started crying: he was hungry. Then Jessie started crying too. I hated myself for not being able to take care of them. I felt as if I was losing my mind.

"Stop crying!" I shouted at them. Their eyes grew wide as they both cried harder and flinched as though I'd hit them. "Oh, I'm sorry, I'm sorry, don't mind Mommy, everything will be all right, Joann will help us and we'll have a nice dinner and a place to sleep." I picked Jessie up and held on to Joey's hand for dear life. Soon the cab pulled up and I sank gratefully into the back seat.

"It's easy," Joann was saying, "you're usually not in

the room more than ten, twenty minutes. Find out what the guy wants before you go into the room and you won't have any hassles. If somebody acts weird, don't go with him. We can work together for a while, do doubles. We won't make as much, but it'll be easier for you until you catch on."

"What about Brad?" I asked, referring to her "man." "I don't want to have a pimp, Joann, I've got kids to take care of. I won't give my money to anybody," I said with finality.

I looked over at Jess and Joe curled up on the couch peaceful and warm. I loved them. My heart seemed to move around in my chest with feelings for them.

"I'll talk to Brad and tell him you ain't choosing him. We'll work a cut with you for your keep and showing you the ropes. He'll go for it—he don't want no more women with kids."

"How much?" I asked warily.

"Maybe forty percent until you get on your own."

"What about Jess and Joe? We can't work with them here, I won't do it!"

"We'll work nights in the motels out by the airport, and I'll still work off the phone during the day. I don't usually have them come here anyway, I usually go to a room to meet them. My regular always takes me out. There's an older woman across the hall, she'll be glad to come and stay with the kids at night. She used to take care of my wife-in-law's kids when she stayed here."

"What's a wife-in-law?"

"It's Brad's other bitch! It's what we call each other when a man's got more than one woman."

"That's not what I am, Joann. We're in partnership, that's all!"

"I know, I know, don't get excited, Trudee. You've

112

got great knockers, the guys will love you. You shouldn't have any trouble pulling tricks."

So, it's what I was born for after all, I thought. I didn't care. To make enough money for the kids and me to live decently, I'd have done almost anything. After all, it had always been a sexual world for me. The boys in school thought they had me. Raymond never believed I was any virgin, and Gary . . . well, I wouldn't pick any tricks that were like him. I shuddered remembering the things he'd talked me into doing. Never again. What I was about to do seemed mild by comparison.

I made up my mind: I'd enter Joann's world and sleep with anyone for the money. Damn it, we'd live well and never be hungry and we wouldn't need help from anyone. I'd take care of my own kids. Fuck the welfare and fuck Gary and fuck the world, which is what I began doing that night.

Joann handed me a red dress with a plunging neckline.

"It's beautiful, Jo, but I'll probably get arrested wearing it."

"Nah, the guys will love it. Try it on."

We were standing in front of her closet. There must have been forty dresses hanging there, all low cut and beautiful.

"Wow, here I'm fixing to get sexy and go out and sell my damn body and my kids are watching 'Road Runner' in the next room. I feel like a creep, a real bad mother, you know."

Joann picked up a jay from her dressing table and lit it. "Don't let it get to you. You're only doing it because you wanna take care of them right. Look, you tried to get help, Trudee, what else can you do?"

"I don't know," I said, sinking into the satin chair in

front of her dressing table. I put my head down on a small clear space between the bottles and lotions and brushes and combs and ashtrays full of butts and roaches. I felt Joann's hand on my shoulder.

"Listen, it's only hard the first time or two. You'll get used to it."

"I hope not," I said, looking up at her.

"Look, what about those square bitches who sleep with their bosses to keep their jobs and end up with a dose of clap and no husband? And I got one guy who tells me he makes it with a stewardess all the time and he pays her."

"Well, I'm sure they're not all like that. At least they can hold a decent job."

"This job *is* decent. Damn it, Trudee, you provide a service and there is damn sure a demand out there for that service. Look, sweetie, if men didn't want to buy sex there wouldn't be any business. All we do is provide it. That's honest, right?"

Beep, beep went Road Runner. I could see their little faces through the doorway, rapt with infant glee over their cartoon. I had to take care of them. I had to make money to get out of Jo's and get a place of our own.

"I guess so, Jo, I don't know any more." I felt weary.

I stood up and pulled on the red dress and looked in the mirror. I looked like a torch singer. Or a whore, I thought.

"Damn, girl! That dress doesn't look like that on me! You're dynamite!"

The young blond woman in the mirror stared back at me. I did look good. The red dress clung to my body and my bust filled out the front perfectly. "I guess I ought to be able to sell something in this number."

"Keep the dress for good luck," Joann said.

"But it looks expensive."

"It is, but Brad buys all my clothes from a fence for a third of the cost. When you start making money, I'll take you to the fence and you can pick out some clothes for yourself."

The babysitter arrived and I kissed the children goodnight. We got into Joann's Buick and we headed out toward the airport, where there would be plenty of businessmen looking for sex.

Joann pulled into the parking lot of the Thunderbird Motel. She drove around the lot a few times.

"What are you doing?"

"Looking for a parking spot by one of the exits. You always find a spot close to an exit."

"Why?" I said warily.

"Don't get excited, it's just good to be near an exit, in case the cops come or the motel manager chases you."

"Oh my God, you mean we might get arrested?" I said, my voice rising.

"Take it easy. I've never been arrested out here, it's just best to play it safe." She parked near one of the rear exits. "Well, let's go."

"Where exactly do we go?"

"We go into the bar and have a drink and wait for a guy to approach us."

"What if it's a cop, Joann? What will my kids do if I get arrested?"

She reassured me. "If there's any dicks around, any vice, the bartender will let us know. The manager out here is pretty cool, and if he knows you work clean he won't bother you. It's just when girls start ripping the tricks off that he gets hot. He knows me pretty well— he only chased me once."

We entered the motel through a side door that led to the cocktail lounge, a nice bar decorated in the "island" theme. It was dark and smoky inside and full of "suits." There were only a couple of women in the place.

I could feel the men leering at us as we walked between the crowded tables and sat down on two stools at the U-shaped bar.

"I'm so nervous, Jo," I whispered.

"Hi, Benny," she said to the dark-haired bartender. "Is everything cool?" she asked, lowering her voice.

"Just fine, baby, no problems. What'll ya have, ladies?"

I breathed a sigh of relief, maybe I wouldn't get arrested tonight.

"Give me a screwdriver, Benny. This is my friend Trudee."

"Glad to meet ya, you workin' with Jo?"

"Hi, I'll have a Cutty Sark and water, please," I said. I looked at Joann.

"I'm helpin' her get started, Ben," she told him. "Don't worry, I'll teach her all the rules."

"You're okay with us, Jo, just stay clean, no robbin'."

As I picked up my drink, I surveyed the men at the bar. Almost everywhere I looked I met a man's eyes. I smiled back suggestiveiy, and then turned away, lowering my eyes coyly.

"Hi, gorgeous, can I buy you a drink?"

I turned on my stool to the voice of a paunchy man in his mid-fifties. Joann gave me the sign: you got one.

"That would be very nice, but drinking isn't exactly what I'm here for," I said.

"How about a drink in my room?"

"Well, that depends." I was hedging. I didn't want to be alone with him.

Jo broke in with a smile. "How would you like to have your pleasure doubled?"

"How much?"

"Well, honey," she cooed, "we could sure give you a

nice party for a hundred dollars." She put her hand on his chest.

"Seventy-five," he said.

"Eighty," Jo insisted.

"I'm on the second floor in the back, Room Twenty-three."

"Why don't you go up now and we'll follow in a few minutes."

"I can't wait to suck on those," he said in an obscene whisper, leering at my bosom.

I felt my stomach turning. Oh God, could I actually go through with this? When he left the room I told Jo how I felt. She reminded me that I had two kids to feed and that nobody gets a free ride.

"You'll see, we won't be in his room more than about fifteen minutes. You'll see how easy it is."

We finished our drinks at the bar and left Benny a ten.

"Do we have to leave him a ten every trick?" I asked as we slipped out the other door of the bar into the corridor.

"I usually leave it two or three times a night, depending on how business is. But he's worth it. He'll also try to line guys up once they've seen us. He probably gets a tip from them too."

We headed down the red-carpeted corridor toward the back of the motel and took the stairway that led to the second floor. Down another corridor and we were at Room 23.

Joann knocked softly while I steeled myself for what was about to happen.

He opened the door wearing only his underwear, so I got a chance to see his flabby belly right away. He lunged immediately for my chest and started groping. I stood there stiff and frozen, submitting.

"Ooh, look at you," Jo said, rubbing his penis. "You look like you're ready for us."

I was glad she touched him, maybe I wouldn't have to.

"Listen," he panted, "my friend, he's just down the hall, he wants somebody too, you could go with him," he said to Jo, "but I'm gonna have you," he said, still fondling me.

"Well, we'll have to get more money, baby," she said, "and he'll have to come up here. We don't work alone."

"I don't think he'd mind, I'll call him," he said, finally letting go of me.

He rang the friend, who knocked on the door a minute later. My trick pulled me down on the bed nearest the door.

"We gotta settle jus' one little thing here, boys," Jo said.

"How much?" the new guy said.

"Fifty apiece, if you're going with us separately. If you each want a round, a hundred apiece."

"I only want to come once," the new guy said.

I felt like I was waking up from a nightmare only to find myself in hell.

They each took out fifty dollars and handed it to us.

"Now," my trick said, putting his wallet in the drawer beside the bed and lunging for me again.

"Uh, take it easy, I'm a human being," I said, trying to smile. "I have to use the ladies' room, I'll be right back."

I saw Jo on the next bed undressing her date. That's what she called it, "date." I thought of a prom date.

I looked in the mirror in the bathroom. The sexy blonde again. Where was the desperate young woman? Forget her, stuff her down. Don't start crying, Trudee,

I told myself. I slipped out of my dress and nylons, and stood with my forehead against the door for a moment. Finally I took a deep breath and walked out to my new job.

He reached for the clasp on my bra immediately. When my breasts fell away he lost it completely. "Oh baby, oh my God they're pretty, oh yes," he moaned pulling me down on the bed.

He climbed on top of me, straddling my body, and began pulling on my underwear. I lifted my hips and let him do what he wanted. Anything to get this over with.

I heard Jo in the next bed crooning to the other guy. "Oh baby, oh, that's right, oh that's good, do it, baby," she lied.

My trick plunged into me. I felt the pain of unwanted entry, the invasion of my nakedness, my intimate me, and I felt a scream of protest welling deep inside. I caught it in my throat and bit my lips. I heard Jo's trick coming as I stared at the ceiling while this guy jumped and pumped at me.

"Oh, yeah, do it," I managed, wanting to shove him on the floor and step on him.

As he exploded inside of me, I kept a vision of the fifty dollars wrapped in my clothes, the fifty dollars I had to have to feed my babies. I hated this man, but I hated myself even more.

His body finally slumped on top of me. It had taken only about ten minutes, but I knew I would feel it forever, would never, ever forget.

Jo was already up and in the bathroom washing. The other man was getting dressed. I moved slightly and the man above me started pumping again.

"Uh, I gotta wash up!" I said, stiffening my vaginal muscles. It worked—his flaccid penis fell out of me. I moved him over and away from me, swinging my legs off the bed and getting up almost in one motion. He grunted again.

"Jo, let me in," I said, knocking on the bathroom door.

She was sitting in the sink as if it were a bidet, scrubbing herself.

"Damn life all to hell," I said, letting the tears fall as I sank down to the edge of the bathtub.

"Oh, it wasn't so bad," she said. "Look, we're done already, we haven't even been out of the bar twenty minutes."

She jumped off the sink and put her hand on my shoulder.

"It gets easier, really. C'mon, let's get out of here, we're missing all that action downstairs. We're gonna have a good night."

"Oh Jo, I, I just don't know if I can keep this up all night."

"Have a double when we get downstairs, it makes it easier."

She pulled down one of the clean white towels and dried herself.

"C'mon, let's go," she insisted, leaving the bathroom.

I washed myself the same way she had. I felt dirty touching myself and yet I needed to wash "him" off of me. My hands were shaking. I'd be better off dead.

I pulled on my clothes and put the fifty in my makeup bag in my purse.

"Hurry up in there," Jo called to me.

I shouldn't have expected much sympathy from her, she'd been doing it about seven years.

When I left the bathroom, my trick jumped off the bed and started mauling me again.

120

"Maybe we'll see you again, baby," Jo said, grabbing my arm and pulling me toward the door.

Down the red corridor again, down the steps and another corridor, into the bar and into the arms of another stranger. I hadn't even known his name. Yet we had just committed the most intimate act performed by human beings—if that's what we were.

Later that night I rolled back the sixth gold hotel bedspread and faced the last strange body for the night.

"Look, I come into Minneapolis every few weeks," the trick said afterward. "Why don't you give me your number and I'll call you?"

"Well, I'm sort of in a temporary situation right now, I'll probably run into you again out here and give it to you then. I should have my own phone by then."

"You're new at this, aren't you?"

"Yes, I am."

"I can tell."

"How can you tell?"

"Just the way you act. You're not so hard. It's quite appealing. Do you have a pimp?"

"Hell, no."

"Good, I hope you don't end up with one. Most of the girls tell me they don't have one, but I know better. Beats me to hell why girls give their money to some goddamn pimp."

"I don't know, it's just not my bag, I've got kids to take care of. I don't need to share my money with anybody."

"Smart girl, stay that way."

I slipped my shoes on and looked in the mirror. The blonde looked tired.

"I hope I see you again," he said, opening the door. "My name's Dick Anderson."

"Hello Dick Anderson," I said shaking his hand, "My name is Trudee." I opened the door and walked back down the long red corridor.

After I paid Brad his cut, I chipped in for food and put the rest away to save for a place of our own. I couldn't believe how much money I had. My mind blocked the ugliness it felt as I scrubbed my body for an hour afterward. If I cried sitting in the tub that night, I forgot about it when I saw my sleeping children warm and safe. I lay down on the floor beside the couch they slept on and pulled a blanket over my weary body.

After I started selling myself I didn't feel I was good enough for anything else. Whenever I found myself in the company of "good" women, I felt I had no right to lick their boots. Yet, their brothers and husbands and boyfriends were my customers. Somehow it didn't feel to me as if it was their fault. I mean, society never looked down on a red-blooded American man for purchasing a little nookie.

It wasn't that I couldn't leave prostitution. Not literally I mean, because I could have gotten a menial job or even sat through the humiliating process of renewing my welfare case. It was more the way I felt about myself. I didn't care enough about my body not to sell it, yet I hated every moment I spent in the strangers' beds. I must have hated myself even more because I didn't stop.

In order to turn tricks I put my mind outside of my body. I just went through it like a mechanical, sexual doll. Bend, stretch, groan, pop.

Once, a trick told me that some girls were toys but that I was a whole playground. That was quite a compliment, yessiree.

"Where we working?" I asked Jo, jumping into her car when she picked me up one night at the house where I now lived with my children.

"Some bitches have been ripping off out at the Thunderbird. It's really hot out there," she said.

"Who?"

"Those bitches of Martin Boyd's—Ginny and Alexis. They're always starting some shit somewhere and blowin' good spots. Brad said I should kick their ass."

"Why doesn't he talk to Martin?" I asked. "It's his problem to keep them in line."

"Sheeet, he tells 'em to rob everybody! He's really an ignorant fucker."

I didn't tell her that as far as I was concerned, all pimps were. They were ugly leeches, sucking money off women. "So where we goin'?"

"Let's try the Ambassador out on the highway."

"I thought that wasn't much of a working place? I don't want to have to worry about the vice squad, Jo, I can't afford an arrest."

"Who can? I met a bartender the other night at an after-hours bar. He said to come out but be very cool."

We found a couple of seats at the horseshoe bar. The woman at the piano was singing "Someone to Watch Over Me." A few people applauded politely at the end of the song. Joann introduced me to Del, the bartender.

"The manager here is really tough," he told us. "You really gotta be cool. There's a guard that usually hangs around by the pool area in the center of the motel, in back. Just stay away from there and watch out for him. I'll tell you if I think a guy is cool here in the bar. There's a couple guys in here before. They went to have dinner. I told them you'd probably be here when they get back."

"Good enough," Jo said. "We'll take care of you, Del."

I looked around the room. Two young couples, fashionably dressed and perfectly coifed, sat at the tables near the end of the bar, laughing and talking and holding hands. I stared at them enviously. How come I was here looking for old men and they were so happy and fulfilled with each other's love?

"Jo, Trudee, I'd like you to meet a couple a friends of mine," Del said as the two men walked up.

The one standing next to me was dark and good-looking, about forty.

"Hiya, good-lookin'," I said, smiling.

"Hello," he said, pairing off with me immediately.

Jo signaled me a few minutes later and took off with the other one.

"What's your name?" the dark man asked me.

"Trudee. What's yours?"

"Vincent."

"Where you from?"

124

"East Coast, Boston."

"I can tell from your accent."

"You seem like a nice person, Trudee. What are you doin' this for?"

"I'll spare you the sob story. I have to, that's all."

We ordered a drink and discussed the price.

"I want a hundred, but I'll stay for a little while, don't worry."

"I'll give you a hundred, but I want you to stay for at least an hour."

"How many times?" I asked.

"I don't care about that so much. Once is enough. It just takes me a while to get going."

"Okay, you go first."

I walked along the corridor to his room wondering what it would be like to be married to Vincent. What if the circumstances were different, what if we'd met in school? Were we so different really? We were just people.

I knocked on the door.

"Hi, pretty," he said, pulling me into his arms. He just held me for a moment. I felt like crying. I reached up and put my arms around him.

"Listen, how about a drink?" he said.

"Sure." I pulled away.

He took a bottle out of his suitcase and poured scotch into two glasses. "I'll go get some ice."

I walked around the room touching his things, his suits in the open closet, his briefcase. What kind of man was Vincent? He probably had a beautiful wife and a couple of kids back in Boston. Why does he need me? He came back and filled the glasses with ice.

"Do you have a family?" I asked him.

"Yes."

"Then why, why me?"

His face grew dark and pensive. "You really want to know?" he said after a pause.

"Yes, I do."

"My wife was injured in an auto accident five years ago. She's an invalid."

"I'm sorry. Do you love her?"

"Yes, at least I love who she was, the memory. It's very hard, living beside her all these years."

"I understand." I did. Here was a man who'd known pain and sorrow too.

Vinnie took my drink and set it on the table by the bed. I wished we didn't have to do this. It was so nice just talking to him. He pulled me down on the bed, unzipped my dress and slipped it off my shoulders. I stood up and let it fall to the traditional motel-gold carpet. He pushed me down again and began tearing at my bra and panties. Then he hurriedly got out of his own clothes and made a dive for me. Oh, I wished we didn't have to do this. He was jabbing at the sides of my private me, so anxious to get it in.

"You're hurting me," I winced.

"Put it in for me, please."

I reached down and guided the stranger inside of me. It hadn't taken him so long to warm up after all. His body jerked, signaling the beginning of his orgasm. I wished we hadn't done it. I wanted to like this man, to feel pity for him, but I couldn't—so he pumped away on a body that was lost to itself forever.

I walked back into the bar and spotted Joann at the far end.

"Give me a drink, Del," I said putting a ten on the bar. A man of about sixty and grossly overweight was staring at me around the curve of the bar. "That guy over there wanna go, Del?" I asked as he set my scotch in front of me.

"Definitely. He asked about you when you left before."

"He better spend some good money, with that body," Jo said dryly.

The man lumbered over to us. "Hi, girls, how about a double?"

"How much you willing to spend?" Jo asked.

"A lot if you do what I want."

"And just what is that?" I asked.

"I wanna see two women together—you two. You don't have to do anything to me, I just watch."

"Oh no," I said, putting a hand up.

"Wait a minute, Trudee. How much will you spend?"

"I'll give you a hundred apiece."

He was breathing heavily. I didn't know if it was from his weight or if he was getting hot already.

"Look, give us a minute. Go finish your drink and we'll send a message through Del, okay?"

As he stepped away, I turned to Joann. "Look, Jo, we've been through this before. You know I don't go for it."

"Trudee," she whispered insistently, "we can pretend. He'll never know the difference. I'll go down on you, you don't have to do it." She was pleading, I knew it was for more than the money. Joann had come on to me before.

The money was good. "Look, Jo, no funny stuff. This will be pretending and that's it, understand?"

"Sure, babe, don't worry," she said.

As we turned the corner of a corridor, we saw the guard and ducked into an exit to hide under the stairwell. The door opened and we held our breath. It closed after a few seconds and he went away.

"Listen, it's no good our walking down this corridor," Joann said, peeping out the exit door. The corridor ran all around the outside of the complex, half of it was wall and the top half was glass windows. "His room is just down there, but if the guard is watching from somewhere he can see the tops of our bodies. Let's crawl. It's only a few feet."

We got down on our hands and knees and crawled along the gold carpet.

"Damn, do I feel silly," I said, bursting into a giggle.

Joann started laughing too, and we stopped for a minute to collect ourselves.

"Ssh, ssh," Joann whispered. "Let's go."

I started forward. All of a sudden, I realized I was crawling over black shoes. I looked up into the face of the old guard.

For a minute no one spoke or moved, then Jo scrambled to her feet. "Let's get out of here!"

I sprang up and we started running with the guard in pursuit.

"If we make it down to Vinnie's room, we can duck in there," I said, praying he was in.

I tapped on the door. "Vinnie, it's me, Trudee."

The door swung open and we made it inside before the guard rounded the corner.

We told him what happened and we all became hysterical laughing. Joann went into the bathroom and Vinnie poured us all a drink. By the time she came out, I had decided I'd had enough for the night. No more chances.

"Look, Jo, I'm spending the evening with Vinnie. We'll hang out here for a few moments and then you can sneak out."

Later Vinnie and I took turns slipping out to his rented car and went to find a nightclub where we could dance and laugh and act like normal people. We almost succeeded. He held me in his arms on the dance floor and I pretended I was his wife or sweetheart. Maybe he did too.

"Come back to my room and stay with me tonight," he begged.

"Oh, Vinnie, I can't. We can't pretend any more, we have to face what it is. I'm a whore and—"

"Ssh," he said, putting his finger on my lips.

"Vinnie," I said, beginning to cry, "our lives are very different and it hurts enough to realize that. You're on the decent side and I . . . well, you know."

"You *are* decent, Trudee, you're decent and good and sensitive. You are."

"Forget it, Vinnie," I said, groping for my cigarettes, "forget it. It's been a nice evening. Please, don't say anything else, please."

He drove me home in silence. Once in a while he'd reach over and grab my hand and give it a little squeeze. "On the right," I said, and he pulled up in front of my house. "Goodbye, Vinnie." I reached for the door handle.

"Wait."

"No, I—"

"You could go away, start over, nobody would know."

"It's not that easy, Vinnie. Maybe you can't understand this, but it has to do with the way I feel about myself. It's very hard to explain. I'm not sure I understand it completely."

"You're worth a lot more than this, Trudee," he said, turning my face toward him.

"You really think so?"

"I know so. Look, I know we'll never see each other again, but I want you to know I wish we could—and not as a business venture either."

"Thanks, Vinnie. Goodbye."

He shook his head sadly. We stared into each other's eyes for a moment. There could have been something there, it was real. Finally he came around the car, opened my door, and walked me to the house like a real date. I kissed him good night, the first time I had ever kissed a trick. It was something you usually didn't do.

I crawled into bed and started crying again. I felt so sad, as if I carried the weight of the world—the sperm of the world is more like it, I thought.

I never forgot Vinnie. Every time I worked the Ambassador his face haunted me. I even turned tricks in the same room. I guess I needed to believe what he'd told me. I hung on to it for dear life.

It was unusual for Gary to call me for anything and even rarer for us to see each other. He was still tending bar, so we knew many of the same people. If we did bump into each other, we were cool and sarcastic. But he made clear that he encouraged my life style; he'd put it down verbally but I could tell that it excited him sexually.

When he came to my house one day I was unprepared for what he asked of me.

"Tell the draft we're still together and they'll change my status."

That would be easy. We still weren't divorced, after four years.

"Are you fucking crazy?" I asked, laughing. "Why

should I help you?" My voice was ice. "You never asked me once if these kids were hungry, and I had to give you a receipt when you bought Jessie a pair of two-ninety-eight sneakers two years ago!"

"C'mon, Trudee," he said, taking my face in his hands. "You gonna hold a grudge?"

"Get out of here!" I was yelling now.

"I'll take the kids away from you! You don't take good care of them anyway. You're a whore!"

"Get out!" I wanted to attack him, blood spun before my eyes.

I was served with papers for a custody suit three months later. I moved to the country near my mother and went on welfare. Jess and Joey attended kindergarten and first grade in the small country school that I had failed to graduate from. I renewed my friendship with Maggie, who lived in the same town with her husband and two kids about the ages of mine.

I settled into a false sense of peace. When the court case came up, I was required to see the court psychologist, a kindly woman in her fifties. I told her about my life and about the love I had for my little ones. I told her about the past few years when I'd sold my body for us to survive. For some reason, I didn't tell her why I'd left Gary in the first place; it felt too personal, I guess.

The fat, smelly old pig that I was blowing to defend me wasn't the best lawyer in town, but I felt I'd win because the kids were loved and clean and always had food and shelter.

All of Gary's relatives came to court and showed a strong family unit. I stood alone fighting for my children. Mama hadn't offered to come with me.

"Mrs. Peterson," Gary's attorney said to me, "is it true that you said to a case worker at the welfare department, and I quote, 'It's people like you who

131

make prostitutes out of women like me'?"

"But that was a year and a half ago."

"Just answer my question, please. Did you make that statement?"

"Yes, but they had refused to give me food or a place to stay. We were in an emergency situation."

He was relentless. "Mrs. Peterson, you've moved fourteen times in the past two and a half years. Why is that?"

"I could never pay the rent on time and—"

"Mrs. Peterson, these photographs are of you, is that correct?"

I looked over the photos of a nude me.

"Wait a minute," the judge interrupted. "Who originally took these photos?"

"Gary. Mr. Peterson."

"Is that true, Mr. Peterson?" the judge asked, looking at Gary.

"Your Honor," Gary's lawyer responded, "that's true, but they were in the possession of another man."

"Close the file, the Court is not interested in the photos."

I felt a moment of relief. But the next witness called was a creepy bartender I'd slept with once, about three years prior to the case. About two years ago I'd helped his wife leave him.

"Yes, I slept with Mrs. Peterson," he testified. "She picked me up in a bar. . . . No, we didn't sleep in the house where the children were, we did it in the car in the alley behind her house."

When the final decree came down, that Gary was to have custody, it was too late to tell them how twisted he was, how dangerous for my children. I was to deliver the children to his mother's house the following Friday, Valentine's Day.

All their little boxes sat in the middle of my living room. "Joey, Jessie. It won't be for long, I promise. And you'll have fun staying with Grandma for a while. She's got such a nice big yard, and Mama will see you all the time anyway," I said with what I hoped was a convincing smile. My heart was ripped in half. Where could I go to hide with them? I had no money since I'd left prostitution. I didn't dare take them on the road— what if I couldn't feed them? Where would I go, how would we begin?

They were crying when I left them that day. I have never done anything more difficult in my entire life than leaving my babies—now five and seven—in the hands of those people who had never cared for them and who took them from me now only because it was convenient for getting Gary out of the draft. He was reclassified 4-F.

I left the countryside and found a room in a cheap hotel in Minneapolis. I contemplated both suicide and heroin and discovered I was afraid of both. I sat in the dark in the small room for days on end, occasionally having food delivered by taxi. I turned a few tricks now and then to pay the rent. Mostly I sat in the dark crying. When my body was used I felt nothing: I wasn't connected to it. It was like a cave in that small room. I stayed high on pills, booze, and marijuana. I just wanted a blank. Feeling was too high a premium to pay at this point.

I didn't call the kids for two months, and I'm still trying to deal with my guilt over that one. I couldn't call them because I was afraid I'd break down if I heard their voices those first two months. I had to try to save my own life first.

* * *

As the old man collapsed on top of me, I felt the tears slide down my cheeks. I wriggled out from under him and went into the bathroom. I lit a joint and took two Valiums. I looked in the mirror: I didn't look twenty-five, I looked forty-five.

I came out and looked around the room. The ancient green shade had a jagged crack in it, reminding me that sunshine existed. Sandwich wrappers and paper cups were scattered around; the sheets were half on the floor; the ugly gray mattress was a glaring accusation of who I was. The trick was zipping his pants, ready to leave.

He came over and mangled my boobs for one final time. "Mmm, you sure got pretty tits."

"Well, sweetheart, you should have pretty tits to play with," I offered, maneuvering his hands off my breasts.

"See you on Friday?"

"Sure."

"Well," he said, looking nervously at his watch, "I gotta get back to work."

"So soon?" I said. I was being sarcastic, but it didn't matter because they heard and thought only what they needed to.

"Don't worry, I'll take care of you again on Friday, baby." He winked as he went out the door.

I picked up and threw my shoe at the door and myself on the sloppy bed. I grabbed a pillow and held it to me. It smelled like him and I shoved it away. I lay there with tears running from my eyes. Soon the new Valiums started working. I got up and lit my joint again, straightened the bed, and lay back down. As I sucked the sweet Panama Red into my lungs, I began to float. Everybody's got to do something, I told myself, and this is what you do best. I got up and counted the money on the dresser. Fucker shorted me a ten. He was a sixty and he had left me only fifty. Well, he had been here for a total of eighteen minutes. The hell with it.

I'd had two tricks that day, earned one hundred and twenty-five dollars. I wouldn't have to see anybody else who called. I had enough money to keep me high and pay the rent for a few days. I poured a glass of scotch and put some tap water in it. I took a large gulp and made a face. I switched on the TV and watched "The Dating Game."

The phone rang.

"Trudee, Joann."

"Hi, girl, whuz up?"

"Boy, you sound fucked-up, girl."

"What's new?" I giggled.

"I got a date for you that pays real good money, but you got to go out of town."

"Now? No way."

"No, this Saturday. Green Bay."

"Shit, those people aren't even alive out there. You mean they see hookers?"

"And how, honey. This guy will buy your ticket and give you two hundred."

"Wait a minute, how come you're not going?"

" 'Cause I gotta see my regular on Saturday. I can't send any of my wife-in-laws 'cause he don't see black girls and I'm the only white one right now. C'mon, Trudee, I know he'd like you, he loves big ones."

That again, and always, forever. "What's the catch, is he a weirdo?"

"Nah, he just don't like to mess around with anything out there, family and business, you know."

"Okay, let me think about it, I'll let you know tomorrow."

"Please, Trudee."

"I'll think about it, Joann," I said testily.

"Okay, okay. It's just that I want to send him a good, clean girl."

For a minute there was silence on the line. "Trudee, you stay in that room too much. I know you're sad now, but staying in that room isn't good for you, it isn't gonna help. Why don't you let me pick you up and take you to the after-hours after I finish work tonight. Come out for a while."

"Sure, mixing and mingling with pimps, listening to their shit all night is gonna make me feel better about my kids, Joann!" I almost screamed.

"I'm sorry, Trudee."

"No, I'm sorry, thanks for trying, I'm just *not* in the mood."

Day after bleak day, the darkness engulfed me and the tricks invaded me. I was usually high within ten minutes after I got up. I might have stayed there forever, or I might have eventually taken my life. I would plan my death in the morning and in between tricks. Always when I picked up the bottle of pills I could see the sweet, beautiful faces of Joey and Jess. I wondered if they'd look the same when they got older. Would they remember me? What would Gary and his family tell them about me? I'd put the bottle of pills down and take only enough to dull my senses.

One day those faces persuaded me to make the phone call.

"Hello, Joey?" I barely whispered.

"Mama, it's Mama! Where have you been, Mom?" his little voice said and I began to feel life flow through me again.

"Well, I had to go out of town and I just got back, honey. I sure missed you and Jessie. Are you all right?" I choked out.

136

"Yeah . . . Mom, are you crying?"

"Well, just a little, but it's 'cause I'm so happy to hear your voice. I love you, Joey."

"I love you too, Mom. When are you gonna come and get us? . . . Wait Jessie, wait. . . . Oh, Mom, say something to Jessie, and then I'll talk to you again."

I held the phone away for a moment and moaned. I couldn't hold it in.

"Mama?" Jessie cried. I could see her bottom lip quivering the way it always did when she cried.

"Hello, baby," I said to my five-year-old. My lip began to quiver like Jessie's. "Oh, sweetheart, I've missed you and Joey so much."

"Are you coming today, Mom?" she begged through her tears.

I made up my mind. "Yes, I think so, baby. Let me talk to your father."

"It was nice of you to finally call," Gary said acidly.

"You don't understand, it's been very hard," I said quietly. "I couldn't." I started to cry openly. "Listen," I said when I got my voice back, "could I take them for the weekend?"

"Where are you living?"

"I don't have a permanent place yet, but I'll get a room at the Ambassador for the weekend. It's nice there and they can swim and everything, okay?"

He agreed. "I'll bring them to meet you in the coffee shop. I want to talk to you anyway."

I would see Joey and Jessie in just a few hours. No more pills. No more booze. (I couldn't give up the marijuana.) I picked out a tailored suit. I wanted to look like a nice suburban middle-class mom, not a hooker.

I got there early and waited in the coffee shop in agony for almost half an hour. They ran to me and I scooped them into my arms. I felt well again. When the children went off to explore the bathrooms, Gary asked me for money. He'd had a speeding ticket and a drunken driving charge. I stared at him contemptuously as I counted out the two hundred and fifty he asked for. I thought if I ever had a pimp (which I didn't), it was Gary. He took the only meaning out of my life because I was unfit, a whore, and now he was begging for the money my broken body made.

After the weekend I tried to stay off the pills, but it was even more desperate than before. I saw their faces constantly. Would they be better off without me? No! I had to stay alive.

Meeting Stanley was a help.

One night Joann and I were out together, having very little luck. We'd been to several hotels around Minneapolis and it was dead, we'd had one date all night. Now we were cruisin' down Hennepin Avenue, the main street of Minneapolis that had all the bars and strip clubs.

"Ain't no fuckin' money out here tonight," Joann said. "Brad'll never believe me. But I'm ready to call it a night. Let's go get something to eat."

We went into an all-night restaurant, where the usual downtown bar crowd was having breakfast—bartenders, waitresses, and die-hards, still trying to convince themselves they were having a good time.

"Stanley's here!" Jo said excitedly. "That guy with the cigar in his mouth. He spends good money and he'll go with two girls too. He used to keep a girl but they broke up about a year ago. Every ho in town has tried to cop him since then, but he don't keep no girls who got men. You oughta try, Trudee."

"I don't think I have the energy."

"He's lookin' over here," she whispered, waving to him.

A waitress came over to us. "Stanley wants to know if you girls would like to join him for breakfast."

"C'mon," Jo said, standing up.

"Jo!" I started complaining.

"Come on! I need at least one more date."

I stood up wearily; I was a little tired of her zest for "the life." I knew it was because of Brad, and it made me sick.

"Hi, Stanley," she said brightly. "I haven't seen you for a long time."

"Who's your friend?" he said, staring at me.

"This is Trudee." She was noticeably disappointed.

"Hi," I managed.

Within minutes, Jo had agreed to go with Stanley's two friends. I was glad to be rid of her.

"You could have gone. How come you didn't?" Stanley asked me.

"I didn't feel like it. Anyway, she needs the money in order to go home tonight, I don't."

"You don't have a man?"

"No, and I don't want one."

"Would you like to go out with me?"

"I don't think so, not tonight. Look, I'm just tired and hungry, maybe some other time. I'll give you my phone number."

"No," Stanley said, "I mean *out*. We'll go to dinner tomorrow night. I'll make it worth your time."

"Okay, sounds good."

I reappraised the fiftyish man. He seemed like a human being. Possibly even good company. He offered to drive me home. We said good night amiably, with plans to go to dinner the next night.

"Play your cards right," Jo told me on the phone the next day, "and you'll have the best sponsor in town."

I told Stanley about the kids at dinner the next night.

It turned out he knew most of the bartenders in town, including Gary.

We were sitting in a nice supper club at a corner table. There was a bottle of Mumm's in a bucket beside the table; the shells from two lobsters littered the table. Stanley knew how to do it right. Nothing cheap for this guy. Including me. I had no idea what he'd give me for the night, or even if we'd sleep together.

"Is there a jewelry store open around here?" he quipped to the waiter.

"At this time of night, sir?"

"I wanna buy my girl here a ring. We're gettin' married in the morning, early."

"Stanley, stop it," I said, laughing. "You're confusing the poor man."

He giggled, his eyes twinkling. The proper waiter smiled weakly.

"He's going to have us hauled away," I said.

"Where would you like to go now?"

"I don't care," I said. I really didn't. I was having a good time. The champagne was making me feel giddy. I didn't feel any pressure to hurry and get "it" over with.

We left the club and drove to one with a piano bar, where Stanley was obviously very well known. The singer smiled at him and a waiter hurried over to our table. I felt a little left out, even jealous.

"Good evening, Mr. Golden, how are you tonight?"

"Fine, Jerry. Give us a bottle of Dom Perignon. My girl here, she's special."

"I can certainly see why, Mr. Golden. I'll have it for you in a minute."

I was impressed, I couldn't help it. I knew some of my tricks were worth a few bucks—those crisp hundreds and fifties they laid on my dresser that told me

140

they were doing all right—but my experiences with them hadn't been like this.

The singer cooed into the mike, "The next song is for one of my favorite men in Minneapolis, Mr. Stanley Golden."

I found myself wondering if he was sleeping with her. "So, you bring me out and other women fall all over you."

"What are you talking about?" he said innocently.

"You're quite a Romeo."

He laughed again, enjoying the atmosphere and attention. The waiter brought the champagne, and I had my first taste of Dom Perignon.

"Ooh, I could get used to this," I said appreciatively.

"I'd like to get you used to it," he said, rubbing my neck.

"What do you mean?"

"We'll see."

We finished that bottle and ordered another one. At closing time we stumbled out of the bar and headed for his car. I rolled a joint from his stash and we smoked our brains out on the way home. All of a sudden I felt nauseated.

He pulled off the highway and I jumped out. I stood behind the car gagging and choking.

"Here," he said handing me a tissue when I got back in the car.

"Jesus, I'm sorry."

"I shouldn't have fed you so much champagne."

"No, it was my fault. I drank it."

"Look," he said when he had parked in front of my house, "I know you don't feel well, so I won't come in."

"No, it's okay, I feel fine now." I owed this man something and I was prepared to pay up.

He handed me two hundred-dollar bills. "Some other time. It's okay."

"But—"

"Just go in and get a good night's sleep. I'll call you tomorrow."

"I'd kiss you good night but—"

He laughed, taking me in his arms and giving me a little squeeze. "Good night."

"Good night, Stanley. I had a good time, really. Thanks a lot. I don't feel right, though, taking this money."

"Good night," he said again.

He called the next day and we made another date. This time he came in and I performed for him. He wasn't so bad, not very demanding in bed and he came quickly. Afterward we lay on my bed smoking a joint. He loved marijuana, and so did I.

"Trudee?"

"Yeah?" I said floating lazily through my high.

"I would like it if you didn't see other men."

"Are you asking to keep me?"

"I guess I am. I'll make sure you have everything you want. Money for the rent, the kids, whatever."

"I won't pretend I love you, Stanley, but I do like you. You're a good man."

"Do we have a deal?"

"Okay."

Stanley was true to his word. I had everything I needed and then some. For the next few months I was with him constantly, although I slept with him only a few times a month. Most of our times together were dining and drinking and partying. Stanley not only took me out but he also took a number of my friends. He was a magnanimous man who liked having an entourage. Besides, we all entertained him. I was fond

142

of him, even loved him in a way. He was like a surrogate father because he protected me, took care of me, and nurtured me. I guess that makes it incestuous, but I needed him then. And because we made love so rarely, I was almost able to forget who I was.

Indeed, I was beginning to feel like a human being again when I was able to visit the kids regularly and to feel stronger about saying goodbye to them when I had to. The aching never stopped, of course, but for their sake I did my best to keep a stiff upper lip. Every Sunday night when they went back to Gary's my heart felt like stone. Soon I started keeping them on Sunday nights too and sending them to school in a taxi on Monday mornings, just to have those extra hours with them. Gary didn't care, I paid him off well for the time I spent with them.

One night when I wasn't seeing Stanley I went with Joann and Brad to a party where everybody who was anybody in the Minneapolis night life was going to be. It figured to be a good place for contacts—all the hookers, call girls, and burlesque dancers would be there with their pimps or "men." Tonight the furs and elegant gowns were taken out and paraded around for each other.

A tall redhead, Electra, joined our table with her escort. She was a beautiful woman and carried herself like a reigning queen. I knew she was a stripper. I'd seen her before at a few after-hours clubs and been introduced to her on one occasion.

I was pleased when she started talking to me. She was somebody important in "the life." Joann was jealous and kept trying to insinuate herself into our conversation but Electra didn't bother with Joann. Strippers rarely bothered with the women who were attached to pimps. If they were taking care of men it

143

was by choice and not because they were slaves.

"Why don't you come down to the club some night? ' the redhead drawled.

"Oh, I'd love to, thanks," I said.

"Good. Why don't we catch a movie tomorrov afternoon. I'd like to talk to you some more," Electra said as she and her escort stood up to leave.

The next day we got high together and went to the movies. We were dressed our usual way, which wa; quite flashy and sexy for an afternoon movie. Electra paid for our tickets with a fifty-dollar bill. "And how did you make that, dearie?" the ticket taker called after us. Electra and I fell out. If we didn't laugh, we could only cry. That's how "the life" is. We sat through two showings of *Cabaret*, then got high again and went to have something to eat.

Electra invited me to the club that night, and that's how I met Cleo—and fell in love. She was one of the most exotic women I had ever seen. Electra and I were standing by the dressing room as Cleo came out in costume: a long orange dress, covered with orange and white beads, that fit her like a glove and a glorious white boa draped over her shoulders. White teeth flashed as her beautiful black face opened in a grin.

"I'm very glad to meet you, Trudee," she said. "Are you a dancer too?"

"Who me? Nooo way, I could never be a dancer." I laughed.

"Why not? You're a beautiful girl and have a lovely body," she said matter-of-factly, her teeth still flashing at me. I was in heaven. She had charisma that you wanted to drown yourself in.

"Electra, we gotta get this girl on stage."

"I agree, Cleopatra darlin'," Electra drawled in that Oklahoma accent. "I thought you'd feel that way."

144

Cleo brought the club owner over and it was settled. She promised him she'd have me on stage the following week. I couldn't believe it: me, a glamorous showgirl like Cleo and Electra. Me, in show business! I'd longed to be an actress all through my childhood. Well, it wasn't Broadway, but it *was* the stage. And it was a nice club with a good band and a comedian-M.C. It wasn't one of the sleazy joints like down the block. It was a step up in "the life" from hooker to showgirl.

When I got home that night I woke up my two hairdresser roommates and told them the news.

I had met Court and Jay through one of the other hookers who had her wigs done by Court. When they found out I was living in a lonely hotel room they took me in and made me theirs. I was their very own private hooker, and Stanley hadn't minded a bit. Now I was their very own private showgirl. They loved it. We sat up half the night making plans for my costumes, my name, everything that we could think of. We talked until they had to dress for work and I smoked a final joint and crashed.

The next afternoon I went to Cleo's house to begin my studies. She had a classy house with fine furniture and a gorgeous white husband. Most of the hookers in town hated her because she had everything they wanted: the best customers, the nicest house, the prettiest body, and the most handsome husband. But I didn't hate her, I adored her. She walked me around the living room in one of her old gowns that day to some strip music. I didn't travel in the same circles as she and her husband, but I'd seen them around town and at a few parties. I'd always been afraid to talk to her because she seemed so grand and elegant—and she was. When her husband came in he took one look and started to laugh.

"You better laugh at yourself," Cleo told him. "This girl's got a job! At least she can support herself," she said, tossing her head arrogantly. "Now get on out of here so she can practice."

He left the room chuckling. I felt like a worm. Why did I think I could get up on a stage and do anything?

"Don't you look like that," she ordered with a smile. "You're gonna do just fine."

When I told Stanley that night he didn't look too pleased. But I did some fast talking. "I've got to have something to do, and I've always wanted to be in show business. You'll see, baby, I'll make you proud of me. C'mon," I wheedled, wrapping my arms around him.

"Why do you ask anyway, you'll do it whatever I say," he said with a crooked smile. "How much is this going to set me back?"

"I just need a few costumes to start out," I said, pouting.

The next thing I knew, it was the night of my first show and Court was fixing my hair.

"Hurry, please," I urged, "Cleo will be here any minute to take me down."

"I'm doing my best, Trudee. Do you want me to do this or not?" he asked testily.

A look from Jay reminded me that Court was extremely temperamental and it wasn't a good idea to make him nervous.

I shut up and continued working on my false eyelashes. "I got goo all over my eyes. I can hardly see, and I still don't have the left one on!"

Jay and Joann, who was there watching too, burst out laughing, which made me laugh.

"Hold still, Trudee, I'm almost done," Court finally said.

I looked in the mirror. I had hair piled up to the roof. I could barely hold my head up. It was showgirl, though, and it was beautiful in the showgirl way.

"It's beautiful, Court," I said, kissing him.

"Now get out there and do it, girl," he commanded.

"Oh God, I'm scared. Oh Lord, how am I gonna get through the first show?"

I heard Cleo's Cadillac honking outside. "I forgot to shave. I didn't shave. My hair will stick out all over the G-string!" I wailed.

Here I was with hair I could hardly carry, one eyelash about to jump off, and my pubic hair hanging out.

"Cleo, I forgot to shave," I said, and I started to cry when I saw her perfectly together self. "I'll never be able to take my clothes off, I know I won't," I slobbered.

"Nonsense, you'll do just fine," she said, handing me a joint. "Here, light this and relax. You've done just fine in practice. After you get through the first show, the rest is easy. Everybody is nervous on her opening night."

"Opening night?"

"Sure, that's what this is, *your* opening night!"

I smoked another joint before we got there and was really starting to feel better. At the club I bolted down two scotches, and it was time for me to go up.

The club was never crowded at the first show, so I would have just a few customers and the staff as my audience.

I'd chosen "My Heart Belongs to Daddy" as my first

trailer. From the dressing room I heard the M.C. announcing me.

"Ladies and gentlemen, we have a treat for you tonight! In her first appearance at the Roaring Twenties, our schoolteacher from Bloomingdale, Miss Trudee!"

The music began as I stumbled out of the dressing room and made the few steps to the stage. The M.C. winked me a you'll-do-just-fine wink as we passed each other. My legs refused to do anything but walk stiffly back and forth. It felt as if there were anchors in them. At the end of the first trailer I somehow managed to get my dress off on time, but it was a miracle. As I draped it over the chair, I realized one of my fingernails was stuck in the zipper. During "Love for Sale," I experimented with taking my nylons and garter belt off, trying to look sexy. The other girls were all sitting toward the back—but I could see them well enough to get some courage—and after every trailer they clapped like mad. Then, during the final trailer, "Night Train," I got my bra off and my bust seemed to fill the whole stage. I looked longingly at the piano, wishing I had it to hide behind. I took my pants off too soon and had a whole song with nothing left to do.

The song went on for what seemed like hours. And I was naked, with just a G-string and pasties on. I was terrified one of my pasties would pop off and I knew my tucked-in pubic hair must have crept out of the G-string by now, even though my movements were slow and stiff. When the music finally ended, I was on the runway, instead of back in the middle of the stage where I belonged for my final bow. I grabbed my clothes and ran off the stage. The girls all gathered in the dressing room I shared with Electra and congratulated me.

"You did just fine," Cleo said, laughing warmly.

"Trudee," Electra drawled, "you gonna be *all* right."

I was shaking. "I took my clothes off too soon!"

"You'll learn to time it. Don't worry about that," Cleo assured me. "You look beautiful on stage."

"I didn't feel beautiful, I felt silly and naked."

The girls all laughed, and then I laughed, and then I felt like a part of them, like I belonged there. It had to be better than flat-backing. At least now, when people asked, I could say I was a dancer instead of a hooker.

For the second show the house was crowded. My legs moved this time and I pranced across the stage like a pro. I teased and taunted and tantalized like the best of them. By the third trailer I had really gotten into it and this time my pants came off just as the last strains of music sounded. I took a bow this time and the audience broke into applause. I had arrived on the strip scene.

Between the shows we had to sell champagne. Cleo and Electra had brought me in on bottles they had sold the first part of the night. Now it was time to solo. I had to walk up to tables and say, "Would you like some company?" Of course, one didn't walk up to tables with women at them, just the singles or groups of men.

I took a deep breath. "Would you like some company?" I asked a man sitting alone.

"Sure," he said. "Want a drink?"

"Yes, but I only drink champagne," I said coyly.

"That's okay," he said ogling my low-cut mixing dress.

"Well, there's a thirty-dollar bottle and a fifteen-dollar bottle. If you get the thirty, I can stay with you longer." I was still too unsure of myself to tell him that the prices actually went as high as two hundred fifty dollars.

"Thirty dollars!" he exclaimed.

"The fifteen will do," I said, losing my bravado.

"Can't you drink something else?"

"I only like champagne. C'mon, we can sit and have a nice long chat," I said, moving closer and squeezing my arms to get an even better cleavage for him to ogle.

"Well," he said less skeptically, unable to take his eyes off my boobs.

"I'd really like to get to know you," I said.

Millie the waitress was there in a flash. "Can I get something for you, Trudee?" she asked, smiling and attentive.

I looked at my victim and batted my eyelash—the other one had just fallen off. "Oh, baby, I'll be right back," I said, grabbing it off the table. I hoped I hadn't blown my first sale.

Electra was in the dressing room getting ready to go on next. When I appeared in the dressing room with one eyelash in my hand and told her it had narrowly missed falling into the man's drink, she screamed with delight. "Here's the glue, Trudee, honey." Earlier I'd borrowed fingernail glue, now it was eyelash glue. I felt like Frankenstein's bride. "Wanna smoke a joint?" Electra asked.

"I'd love to, I could really use it, but I better go back and see if I can salvage this bottle. I haven't sold any on my own yet."

"I'll leave you a roach under the Kleenex box, baby, smoke it later. But rub oil on the light bulb before you smoke—use this Jungle Gardenia bath oil of Cleo's, you can't smell nothin' else."

On the table was a bucket with the coveted bottle of champagne. I wasn't too late. Millie was opening it. Pop it went, like the next thousand I would sell. As I sat down, she poured me a glass.

150

"I'll get you a glass of fresh water too, Trudee," she offered, and she returned with a tall Tom Collins glass. This, the "spit-back" glass, contains only ice and a drop of water in the bottom, but the customer can't see this in the dark. The idea is to take a swig of champagne, hold it in your mouth, pick up the "water" glass, and, while pretending to take a drink, spit back the champagne. This is fine for experienced practitioners, but that first night every time I took a drink I somehow timed it wrong, as I had my last peel in the first show, and ended up swallowing much more often than spitting.

After three fifteen-dollar bottles with the customer (he hadn't saved any money after all!), I was feeling pretty good. And I had buckets, literally, of courage. On my last show I really outdid myself. I started swinging and swaying my number-one assets around like an old-timer. When I got off stage, Millie came and knocked on my dressing-room door, to inform me there was a customer waiting to buy me a bottle.

Cleo, Electra, and I scored hundred-dollar dates at the end of the night and took off in Cleo's car for the suburban motel they were staying at. It took us longer to drive there than to turn them. After we were finished, Cleo went home to get her beauty sleep and Electra and I rolled her Cadillac over to an after-hours club to meet Court and Jay. It wasn't the pimp-type joint but mostly gays, fag hags, and bi's. We popped a couple of black beauties and smoked a half a pound and danced and rocked and laughed all night. Court and I rarely missed a song and poor Electra got stuck dancing with Jay, who never danced but stood on the floor snapping his fingers off-beat and asking me a million questions about my customers. I'd sold—and *drunk* most of—a hundred and fifty dollars' worth of wine that night. Electra had sold three hundred and drunk half of it. Cleo, though, had sold four hundred and drunk none: she was a business woman, Electra and I were party girls.

I avoided seeing tricks after the show as much as possible. I had my salary and a cut-back on the champagne, plus the money Stanley gave me, which kept me pretty well. I had more money that I knew what to do with, even after paying for my own necessities and pleasures and everything I could think of for my own children, as well as payoffs to Gary. But somehow I spent it all. I loved/hated the money, loved it because I could earn that much, hated it because how I earned it made it dirty money. Piss it away, there's more where it came from. I gave it away, loaned it out, and in general felt I had to take care of the down-and-out of the world. Hadn't I been there once? Sometimes girls came to me who had pimps and hadn't made enough for the night and were afraid of a beating when they got home. I "loaned" them enough to fill their quota, knowing of course I'd never see it again.

Court, Jay, and I sometimes sat up half the night in my bed eating and smoking. My bedroom looked like the back alley of a take-out joint. We sat among dirty plates and food wrappers, laughing at life and avoiding the real world.

One Sunday I came home from lunch with Stanley to find Court waiting on the stoop. "Trudee, I've got something to tell you," he said nervously.

"Shoot."

"You know all those new shoes of yours?" The week before I'd bought six new pairs of shoes ranging in price from forty to eighty-five dollars.

"Yeah?" I said.

"Well, uh, Fatty Pig ate them." Fatty Pig was an

152

English bulldog that belonged to Jay who was upstairs hiding under the bed with him.

"I'm a whore, I'll buy some more!" I said flippantly.

Court howled. He told that story all over town in all the gay bars—it's still one of his favorites.

That's who I was, a money-makin' whore. Things had no value. Especially me.

Soon I was no longer opening the show at the club but had been moved to fourth place, which meant that only Electra and Cleo went on after me, that I was feature material. My shows were getting much better, I could tell by the applause and the amount of champagne I was selling.

Everything up to now had been fine with Stanley. Then he made a mistake: he fell in love. He began following me around when I wasn't with him, which made me very angry, and we began fighting over small, inconsequential things. I had to feel I had a life apart from him, even though he was paying well for my time with him.

"I guess you won't want to be seeing me any more," he said one night.

"Well, it's up to you, Stanley."

It was the end of our relationship. I ran into him now and again when I was out and about. We sort of looked at each other wistfully, both sorry it had gone the way it did. I missed him, not just the money, but because he had become a friend, or as close as you can come to friendship under the circumstances.

Now I had to take more tricks to keep up my life style, and of course I hated it. Just because I was a showgirl, it didn't make sex with tricks any better. Actually, I could delude myself only so much: when I wiggled and paraded myself on stage, I was a piece of meat available to the highest bidder. But I had decided to stay alive.

I moved to a small house on Cedar Lake and settled in to a life style that few people will ever know.

In order to see my children on weekends and during their school vacations, I had to pay my dues to Gary in the form of sex and money.

The rest of my private time I started spending almost exclusively with gay men, particularly Court and Jay. They didn't want my body, they were good friends, and I always had an escort and someone to get high with. Those days I stayed high except when Joey and Jess were with me. And when I wasn't at my job or turning tricks, my buddies and I started going with a new crowd of about a dozen gay men and six women. They were glad to have an exotic dancer in their midst and we became a "family."

Like so many other people who banded together to take drugs (with them I had my first experience with several new ones) and talk about gurus and the war, we needed each other to survive the bad trips and the sixties. We got together on Friday nights and all dropped acid or psilocybin or mescaline. And the family grew. A comfortable circle, we felt we were experimenting with drugs together to raise our consciousness, so we all invited a friend. I brought all the strippers in and the gays added their lovers or friends and the women added their friends. Everybody wanted to turn someone else on.

My house was big enough for everybody and we often ended up there. If I had to work, I would take my tab of whatever after my last show and, at 1 A.M., jump into a cab and get home where the "family" was already high and full of love. We spent the night holding each other and talking about anything. We felt very good. In the early morning everybody would be crashed around my house, sleeping in little bundles. I'd walk through the bodies and debris of wine bottles and ashtrays and look lovingly at them. By the time people started waking up, it was afternoon. Somebody would go to the store, and somebody would cook, and some of us would clean up. After we ate, we'd drop another hit of something and start again. We were desperate for the glow.

When we discovered M.D.A. we couldn't get enough of it. When our dealer from Madison, Wisconsin, came into town with a new supply, someone got on the phone and called everybody in the family. It meant an immediate party. M.D.A. had the most incredible effect. When you started getting off, this golden glow would begin in your chest and spread to all parts of your body including your toenails. Every part of your body was on call to love. Not in the exploitive way that had been so much a part of my life for so long, but with a warmth that I had never experienced before. It made you think you were in heaven, ready to hold a bum in your arms, no matter how down-and-out and how disgusting he was, because he was one of "the children." And your friends, you *couldn't* love them enough. It felt as if it would be impossible to hate anybody, including myself. We wanted to feed it to the whole damn army and navy, on both sides. Unlike acid or even mescaline, its only properties were love. It was a pity that we had to get it from a drug, but we were so alienated and starved for love that we were grateful to get it at all.

For me, drugs became the first step out of "the life," because when they didn't work any more, when you took so much you blitzed out your brain and *still* couldn't forget, then you were either going to get the hell out or end up dead.

The other steps were harder to take, but I was on my way to feeling better about myself. Of course it didn't hurt to get a little push now and then from something so hateful you'd never want to go through it again. Like the strain of Vietnamese gonorrhea I caught from one of my regular tricks who owned a greasy spoon and slept with a waitress whose husband had just been home on furlough: three weeks in the hospital and all chances of ever having another child wiped out.

Even that, however, was not as powerful a force as Pete, another "sponsor" Cleo was arranging for me.

"But he's such a gross pig," I argued. "I mean really unattractive. I saw him last month, remember."

"Trudee, he's a good sponsor and you need the extra money right now," she reminded me.

I'd hired another lawyer to try to get custody of the children. He was expensive, she was right. And practical, as usual. Sponsors were few and far between; I hadn't had one since Stanley.

"You know how hot things have been in town lately. Hardly anybody has been making any money," Cleo continued.

"There's some money," I said, pointing out the car window at six well-dressed businessmen walking out of a hotel. "Fifty, a hundred, a hundred and fifty . . . three hundred," I said, counting their potential worth.

Cleo laughed. "You wait till the street girls approach

them. Watch some morals squad officer come out of nowhere."

"It's not that I don't appreciate your fixing me up, Cleo—I do. And I guess I have no choice. I'll try it for a while. Give him my number."

Pete called me the following week. He came to town only twice a month—maybe I could stand it. After all, I'd done everything else. He called almost two hours early the first time. Well, I'd be damned if I'd spend two extra hours with him. A deal is a deal. I ignored the ringing. When it stopped I peeked out the window. I saw Pete walk to his rented car, climb clumsily inside, and pick up a newspaper. He was going to wait for me. Now I was trapped.

After forty-five minutes he finally pulled away. In the meantime I had taken two Valiums and smoked a joint so I could get high enough to deal with him. In twenty more minutes the phone rang.

"Hello," I said after the seventh ring.

"Hi, baby, it's Pete. Where have you been?"

"I just got in. I wasn't expecting you for another hour."

"I got an earlier flight. I couldn't wait to see you."

Goody. "Well, I can be ready in about a half an hour."

"See you then, honey."

I smoked another joint.

When he arrived he put his arms around me and tried to kiss me. He had a peculiar odor I couldn't identify.

"Would you like to go to lunch?" he asked, rubbing my ass.

In the car, he kept grabbing my leg. His fingers were so pudgy they looked more like toes.

"Take it easy, you're hurting me," I said, trying to keep the anger out of my voice.

During lunch, he continued grabbing my leg under the table. His hands were insistent, demanding: I was bought and paid for.

"I can't wait to get my hands on you," he said, panting, in his hotel suite.

What did he think he'd been doing the last two hours in the restaurant and in the car?

"C'mon over here, baby," he said from the bed. He pulled me down on the blue satin bedspread, groping and clawing at my breasts. His ugly hands pinched and pulled and squeezed.

"Take it easy, Pete, you're hurting me."

"I'm sorry," he gasped, not letting up one bit.

Then it was, Do this, do that, touch me here, do it that way, do that again. It took me what seemed like hours to get him up. I felt like the hole of the world as I continued to try to give him pleasure. It was my job.

Oh Lord, please make him come, I said over and over in my head.

"Now, baby, I'm coming now," he gasped finally. "Do you feel it? Are you coming too?"

"Yes," I lied. I thought I was going to lose my mind right there on that goddamn blue satin bedspread. Finally, mercifully, he rolled off me. I jumped up and ran into the bathroom.

"You dirty whore," I said into the mirror. "You're just a dirty, filthy whore." Why am I doing this? What else can you do?

That night we repeated the procedure, except it took longer because he was drunker. He kept trying to kiss me and slobbered all over my face. A few times I almost threw up on him. Then I thought of my attorney's fees.

The next morning he said, "You are something else.

Let's take you shopping for something pretty."

Did I have to walk around in a store with him too?

He took me to one of the most exclusive stores in Minneapolis. He sat on a chair in the showroom while I modeled dresses for him.

"I like that on you," he said when I tried on a jump suit and matching maxi-coat that was fashionable at the time. The coat had a beaver collar and a matching muff. A beaver muff! How appropriate. Three hundred and seventy-five dollars.

"How about some perfume?" he said next, pulling me by the arm. I wanted to pull away, shake him off, and run out of the store. The saleswomen were whispering behind us—they knew who I was, all right.

When we pulled up in front of my house he grabbed me again. "Did you have a nice time with me?"

"Yes, of course," I said, ready to jump out of the car.

"I'll see you next week. Same time?"

My heart sank. Next week?

"Oh," I said, hardly able to contain my disappointment, "I thought you could only come in every other week."

Like the others, he heard what he wanted to. "Will you miss me?"

"Sure. I better go, uh, I have a lot to do before work tonight."

"Okay. Here," he said, reaching into his pocket, "something to tide you over." There was two hundred and fifty dollars in his toelike fingers.

I hated reaching for it. "Thanks, baby," I said, giving him a quick kiss on the cheek and leaping out of the car.

I bathed again and again and again. I couldn't take this, no matter how much money he gave me.

"Did Pete take good care of you?" Cleo asked later.

"Well, he spent good money."

"Good. I told you he would."

I could never be as pragmatic, as objective, as Cleo. I knew I had to get rid of Pete and pay the lawyer off another way.

It wasn't much, that decision, but it made me feel a little better. I might be a whore but I was also a human being; I was becoming more and more certain of it.

I wasn't exactly ready to go out of business altogether, but I had learned how to build in some limits. For example, I didn't mind seeing Jim—even though his secretary announced me as "the bottom line on your expense account" when I phoned him at his office—because sex wasn't a big thing to him, he just loved being around hookers. And he did buy me lots of things and sometimes took me to Vegas, where I played the one-armed bandit and heard Elvis and Paul Anka. But I was getting rid of the repulsive ones, the ones who said things like, "Oh, I can't wait to do it to you, little lady," and then jabbed and jabbed at me until they had to plead, "Put it in for me." I was finally sending them—and their hundred dollars—away.

Joey and Jessie continued to be my only reality. I lived to be with them. It was still the only time I wasn't high, the only time I could stand not being high.

They had begun to notice things about Gary that really scared me.

"Mama, why does Dad lock himself in the bathroom and stay so long?"

"What are you saying, Joey?"

"He goes in there and stays and stays and he's got all those magazines under the sink."

"What kind of magazines are they?"

"Funny stuff," Jessie said, "with women kissing each other *all over!*"

160

"And stuff with animals and people," Joey added. "It's disgusting!"

"Do people really do that, Mom?" Jessie asked.

I sat them down then and talked for a long time, telling them as much as possible to make them understand the sicknesses of adults. It was hard, they were only seven and nine.

Poor children: a hooker for a mother and a pervert for a father. They sure lucked out. I had to change, I had to make things different for them, I had to get them away from Gary. I might not be a prize, but they would probably be exposed to less sexuality living with me than living with their "straight" father. At least I had always kept my business away from them.

But the more I was away from them, the more drugs I took, and the more drugs I took the more sensitive I became. It was becoming impossible to lie under a trick.

The last time I had opened my eyes to see the sagging flesh of the old man's shoulder flapping in my face. I started to gag, then turned my head into the pillow and bit into it to keep from screaming. I was crying but I didn't want the trick to know. I was afraid he'd stop and I'd have to start all over from the beginning, and I knew I couldn't.

Often I was too high to do my job at the club well. And I was even beginning to feel guilty when a man spent, say, sixty dollars on a magnum of champagne and I spit it out. I had to get out before I lost my mind— I was beginning to feel as if that were really a possibility.

And then I met Jimmy Star.

I'd seen him in the gay bars, on the fringes of the crowd a few times. He was tall and handsome and had a beard. I've always had a weakness for face hair; I guess it appeals to the little-girl-who-lost-her-father in me.

Jimmy was a hairdresser, like many of the gays, but he was also studying Jung at the university. Whenever he showed up at our parties, he and I would go off into a corner and talk and talk. He lent me all his books on Jung and encouraged me to read them. He talked about serious things to me and treated me as if my opinion was worth listening to. Occasionally, I thought I saw something other than friendship in his eyes—maybe it was because I wanted to see something. Mostly, I tried to relax in the friendship and enjoy it. I was very lonely when he went to Mexico for a while.

I was rushing to get on the stage, late as usual, with "My Heart Belongs to Daddy" starting, when my dressing-room door opened and there stood my step-father's grandson.

"Trudee," he said, "your mother is dead."

My "NOOOOOOOOOOOOO!" rose above the noise of the crowd and the music. Cleo and Electra came running.

I remembered hiding behind her skirts when I was little. Now there would never be a place to hide again.

We were standing by a jewelry counter in a store in Minot, North Dakota. I stood staring at the pretty things behind the glass. All of a sudden I looked up and the familiar blue dress wasn't there. In its place was a yellow dress. Panic seized me as I realized my mother was gone. In a four-year-old's terror I looked

162

wildly around the store. Where was my mother? I started sobbing.

"Get him away from me!" I screamed. "Get him away! He's lying. Oh my God, Cleo, my mother. NOOOOOOOOOOOOOOOOO!"

Cleo had me in her arms and was giving orders to the other girls to get someone up on stage immediately. The music was still playing my first trailer.

The grief was an ache, a welling pain that felt like my insides would burst with it. Oh Mama, you never had a good life. It was such a hard life and you wanted things so simple. Poor Mama.

Poor Trudee. If Mama was gone, who would be the mama?

The last time I had talked to her was when I called to tell her I was going to be on television.

"On the ten-o'clock news," I said proudly.

"Well, my baby on the news. What are you gonna be doing?"

"They're filming some clubs getting ready for New Year's Eve, and they're showing all the dancers prancing around on stage. Don't worry, Mama, we all have bathing-suit-type costumes on," I assured her, referring to what we never talked about or admitted.

"I'll be watching," she said, sounding relieved.

"Mama, it was a nice Christmas," I said. I had taken Joey and Jessie out to visit her and my stepfather was the warmest he had ever been to us. "It was really nice. Thank you."

"It made me happy too, toots. It really made me feel good that everybody got along finally." It was a coup for Mama, and she felt as if a great burden had been lifted from her shoulders.

"I love you, Mama. Happy New Year."

163

"I love you too. Happy New Year. Be a good girl, toots."

"I will, Mama."

Mama's death changed something inside of me. I felt older, more responsible. Now I was the mama. I had grown up overnight. Now there could be no excuses for my life. It had to change, and fast. I wouldn't have forever; my own mortality faced me menacingly. Would Joey and Jessie continue to grow up with a whore for a mother? Be a good girl, toots. I will, Mama.

I stopped dancing and hustling and just sat alone in the little house on Cedar Lake, getting high and thinking, thinking. Who was I? Hooker, mother, person?

Cleo came, and Court and Jay and my other friends. They all tried to help me pull it together. I didn't have the courage or energy or something. I started thinking about suicide again.

How could I get out of "the life"? What would I do then? Who would accept me? How could I change all my friends and the only thing I knew?

Court and Jay fell on hard times and moved in with me. It helped to at least have other bodies occupying the space, but it was a cruel winter and none of us had work. Since we couldn't pay the bills, the gas and electricity were turned off. I called the company and asked to speak to the manager. I propositioned him, and by that afternoon I had heat and lights and the manager in my bed. I felt helpless to do anything else.

Cleo finally persuaded me to go back to dancing, this time on the road. "You've got to stay busy," she said, "and the clubs in Green Bay, Madison, the outlying cities, pay good money for a feature like yourself. You can headline at any of them."

I went to work in Appleton, Wisconsin. I didn't see many tricks, but I did let men take me to dinner and lunch as often as possible to save money. The rest of the time I sat in my lonely hotel room crying. Was it true, as pimps used to say to me, "Baby, the only people ever gonna love you is a pimp and a trick"?

I went back to Minneapolis and started dancing there again. I started tricking again too. I just couldn't go without the money. I was giving Gary a lot of money and was afraid if I didn't the kids would go without something. I was trapped. I knew I had to, *had to* leave "the life" but I didn't know what else to do. I would pick up the newspaper and stare at the help-wanted column. What could I do?

Receptionist wanted; must be neat and attractive.

They would be able to tell. I wasn't neat, I was sexy. It was all I had ever been.

"Tell me, Trudee," they would ask me, "what jobs have you worked at?"

"Uh, blow jobs."

I was afraid of that world. They were all so nice and clean and I wasn't. So I turned tricks and put away the money.

When Jimmy Star came back from Mexico, he helped me pick up the pieces. We got to know each other's hearts. He kept urging me, "Trudee, you're a good person. You deserve more than this. You have something better to give the world."

The concept was new to me, frightening but exciting. If someone as good as Jimmy could feel that way about *me*, maybe it was true. I had always harbored secret

feelings that I was meant for something good, something special. I had been afraid to voice these feelings,
to let them surface, but now with Jimmy's encouragement, his faith in me, I formed a very small but hopeful
vision of the possibility of a different life style.

I wasn't turning many tricks. Whenever I did, it
upset me for the day. I wasn't able to block out my
feelings any more. In order to turn tricks you have to
keep your mind and body separate. And it's impossible
to grow that way, always separated from yourself. I
had begun, through the trauma of Mama's death and
through my time with my children and through
Jimmy's friendship and caring, to be less separated.
Turning tricks was beginning to be impossible.

Ironically, it was a gay man who finally showed me
the love and self-worth that other men had taken from
me. Jimmy and I took a lot of trips together, and I
began to try seducing him. I worked at being subtle
about it, and the scheming began to get tedious. I
wanted him in a different way from any other man. I
wanted to drown in his gentle intelligence. He wrote
me poems and brought me flowers but never touched
me in a sexual way. I was surprised I had those
feelings, so new to me.

The most important thing Jimmy did was to keep
telling me how good I was and to treat me as a person
worth something. I fell in love with Jimmy Star because
through him I was beginning to love myself.

We had good times together, laughing and loving,
but we didn't make love, Jimmy couldn't. Every time
we tried, he froze. It just didn't work. We spent a lot of
time together and I kept trying, gently, carefully. I
don't think I had ever wanted anybody so much.

He was overjoyed that I had given up hustling.
When the tricks called I said, "Sorry, baby, scratch my

166

number, this body is not for sale!" It felt *so* good. Sometimes Jimmy would answer the phone and tell them they had the wrong number or that I was married. Then we'd laugh and dance all over the house.

Those months were incredible—no tricks, no dancing. The only thing that hurt any more was not having the kids with me permanently . . . and the memories. Jimmy helped me with the memories. We meditated, we danced, we laughed, and, my God, did we share.

"Where do you want to go?" he asked me one evening.

"Not a gay bar," I said. "Let's go to a straight place." I waited for him to say no.

"All right, you got it."

Maybe if I could get him away from other gay men, we could make it happen.

Locked in each other's arms on the dance floor, no drugs, just a bit of booze, he was holding me, really hanging on to me.

"You little shit," he said surprised, happy, "you've got me horny!"

We went home and made love till the wee hours of the morning. In the dark, with a candle, he looked at me all over. "Is this what I've been so afraid of?" he said, laughing.

"Oh Jimmy, you were wonderful!"

"Was I?" he said proudly.

I still hadn't felt much, even with Jimmy, whom I'd wanted so desperately. Perhaps I never would. But it was good making love with Jimmy, warm and tender and everything it wasn't with the tricks.

We didn't do it very often as neither of us seemed to need sex a great deal. We needed each other, and helped each other work out our different and painful feelings: he didn't want to be gay and I didn't want to be a whore. Through our mutual acceptance and love, we began to be strong enough to make changes in our own lives. We groped at the strings of each other's hearts. It was an intense relationship, with much at stake for both of us—but not together. We knew that that wouldn't have worked. We were passage people for each other.

Jimmy Star and I would remain close friends in the years to come. There was a bond between us. Every time we see one another, even after long absences, the close feeling is there.

When the opportunity came—strange as it was—for me to get away, I was strong enough to accept it. A man I had met in Appleton had kept in touch. He wasn't a trick, but he did come to watch me dance, bought me champagne, took me out for meals, and gave me money. He had three little boys and a wife who was institutionalized for severe emotional problems. Sam was so lonely and sad that I thought of him as someone whose life was as miserable as mine at that time.

Sam came to see me in Minneapolis. No sex; he needed my friendship, he said, not my body.

"Trudee, what would you like to do with your life?" Sam asked me. "Would you like to go to school? What kind of work do you think you might eventually like to do?"

"Don't laugh at me, please," I said, feeling a little shy and embarrassed, "but what I've always wanted to do is study theater."

"I'm not laughing. Where could you do that?"

"I guess I'd have to move to New York."

"I think you'd be very good," Sam said. "When would you like to leave? I've been wanting to take the boys and get away from this area myself."

He had taken me by surprise. But suddenly it all seemed to make sense. Sam said he wanted to be near me, although he knew I didn't feel anything sexual for him. His kids were most important to him, and they badly needed a surrogate mother—which service I was pleased to provide. Of course, my kids were most important to me, and their father was drinking pretty heavily now. This could be my chance to snatch them and take them with me.

Sam was very sympathetic. "What if I send you on ahead and you get situated and then you just take the kids. What will Gary do?"

"I don't know, I guess I'll find out when I do it," I answered, feeling more and more excited by the prospect. "But I've got to get them away from him. He really scares me—and worse, he scares them. They know he's weird, they ask a lot of strange questions."

The plan was set. I prepared to leave. I hadn't told Joey and Jessie yet that I was going to take them. I didn't dare. So it was like ripping my limbs off to say goodbye. I promised them I would see them in a few weeks. I couldn't stand the looks on their faces, but I had to keep my secret from them for a little while. Soon they would be with me for good and I would make it up to them. "I love you with all my heart!" I wept, taking them in my arms. "I'm not going away, you'll see."

They trusted me with their eyes, but their hearts were broken that Mama was leaving, even for a while. In New York, I registered for acting classes and began looking for an apartment.

I guess I should have known, even then, that such a complicated plan, with so many tenuous props, was doomed to at least partial failure. Of course, it became even more complicated than I could have dreamed at the time, but it did get me away from the dead-end existence I had been locked into for so long.

And it did—at least indirectly—get my children back with me. It had turned out that Gary's drinking and violence with them and with his girlfriend were worse than I had imagined. When Joey and Jessie told me that they were frightened to the point of running away, I took matters into my own hands. I actually tried persuading the acting judge in the custody suit four years before, but he simply sent a message that I'd have to get a lawyer and petition the courts to make any change. So I obtained permission to take them out of state for Thanksgiving—and I kept going, all the way to New York. And wouldn't you know it, Gary made practically no effort to get them back.

For a while after Sam and his three boys joined us, things were pretty good. Unfortunately, Sam's expectations of me began to change a few months later. Soon he made it clear that he could no longer tolerate the absence of a physical relationship, and I just couldn't tolerate the thought of the presence of one. Finally, Sam took his children and left. It was extremely difficult to lose what I had gained with those little boys, and it meant I was losing our means of support too. But at least I knew even better what my personal dignity felt like.

Joey and Jessie and I had some rough times—like when I lost my waitress job (I never did quite make it as an actress) because I broke my leg, and we had to go on welfare. And we had some fun times—like finding out what good friends we had when they let us camp out in their loft when we were between apartments. But, most important, we were together. In New York, the first place I had ever felt truly at home.

170

After a few years, we had to make another change. The kids were young teenagers now and their rootlessness in the big city was beginning to worry me, and I had become involved in a complicated love affair (at least it was a *real* love affair). So it was time to get out. Back to Minneapolis, where else?

It was good to be with Cleo and Court and Jay and Electra. Jay had opened a beauty shop and Court worked there with him and Electra was in beauty school. Cleo was the one who had made it out successfully and opened a small boutique. Some of the other girls were still dancing and looking pretty rough. The good clubs had closed or gone over to the topless go-go scene and become very sleazy. Some of the old crowd were taking junk and drinking themselves to death. I knew I hadn't worked my life out yet, but I was trying, and suffering through the changes necessary to really make it different.

Jessie hated it there and, despite my distress, decided to go and live with her father. I took a job in a Chinese restaurant and, with Joey, moved into a small apartment, where I became good friends with the two nurses who lived downstairs. They were twin sisters, my age, who left their husbands simultaneously and decided to move in together, with their four daughters, two each. We shared a lot of good things, disappointments, goals, tears for broken lives and joys for new hopes. We also shared our fears for our children.

Jane's daughter Babs, fourteen, was flirting with the popcorn pimps that the city was rife with. Mary's daughter Linda was taking a lot of acid and playing hippie. My own Jessie, living with Gary, had begun to take the killer—angel dust. Who were we? How had we fucked up so badly? What dreams had we bought that broke us so when they weren't true?

171

In fact, I was worried to death about Jessie. I knew angel dust was the worst drug around, next to heroin. I'd smoked it once and vowed never again to touch it. It was dangerous crazy stuff and very available in Minneapolis. I felt that she had turned to the drug because of her confusion at being with her father, who was still an alcoholic, drinking himself to death, and whose deterioration had become quite evident to the kids.

Out of frustration at not being able to get through to Jessie and out of my very real concern, I started talking more to Jane's and Mary's daughters downstairs. I even took Jane to a pimp bar so she could see the life Babs was playing with. I talked to Linda about acid and, when she tried to run away to California, found her in a crash pad in southeast Minneapolis and brought her home.

"I don't know what you're doing working in a Chinese restaurant when you're so good with kids," Jane said one day.

"If I'm so good, how come my daughter is on angel dust?" I asked glumly.

"I guess it's more difficult to help our own sometimes because we're too close. But I think you'd be very good counseling, Trudee," Mary added.

"So who's going to hire an ex-prostitute? I mean, no degree, folks."

"Oh yes, you have a degree," Mary insisted. "You've been there!"

Jane got in touch with a woman she knew at the Hennepin County attorney's office who had been working on the problem of juvenile prostitution. June Fleeson said yes, she would like very much to meet me, and an appointment was set up.

I liked her right away. She had a bright honest face and was completely open and intelligent. I could already feel that she would not judge me, but weigh everything I told her carefully.

When I finished my own story, I talked about why I thought girls got into "the life," why they were vulnerable to it. "In spite of the radically changing attitudes about sex and morals," I said, "I really don't think suburban and country girls from this area are very sophisticated about street life. When they run away and are approached by a man, they have no idea he's a pimp. They just see the flash—"

"What?" June interrupted.

"Sorry." I laughed. "I forget that people aren't familiar with the lingo. 'Flash' means the diamonds and other jewelry a pimp wears. Anyway, they see the flash and the three-piece suit and the big Cadillac. They think he's some hot shot from New York or the West Coast. They're terribly naïve about a pimp-rap. You know it's awfully easy for a person to assume these girls are stupid, but I don't think that's true at all. They're lonely, hungry, and most of all naïve. A pimp will tell a girl she's fine and she's star potential and she could be rich beyond her wildest dreams and wear the finest clothes, go to the best places, make her really feel important, and build up her ego. Now what fourteen- or fifteen-year-old girl doesn't want to hear that?"

June nodded. "I think everybody needs to hear—or wants to hear—positive talk. Adolescents are usually pretty insecure anyway. If they're on the run, that need must be heightened."

"That's it." I was thrilled to have the opportunity to discuss these things so sensibly with someone. "I think a pimp feeds a girl's fantasy, whatever it is—love, power, money, control, the good life. Once he gets her nose open—"

June looked at me quizzically.

"Oh. That means get her to fall for him, become infatuated. Once that happens, he puts her on the street—turns her out, as they say. He usually tells her it's just for a little while, but of course that's not true. If she doesn't go for it, she gets beaten, raped, and drugged. I know it happens a lot, but more often I think it's just the art of persuasion. You'd have to hear these guys in action to appreciate the psychology of it. They're *very* good at what they do. A girl who is white, lower or middle class, from a rural or suburban environment, probably feels degraded or lowered on the social scale after having sex with a black street person. She may not be totally conscious of all the feelings involved, but it's going on inside of her. She might act like it's cool, but that's not what she really feels."

"Wow," June said, "my head is spinning. I'd like to have some time to think about it all. It's really powerful."

I so much hoped I'd be able to work in this area. "Do you think I could really help and also find a job, which I need," I asked her.

"I'm certain that you could help," she said. "There's just too much we don't know about that world. And the girls don't really tell us much. They see this person across the desk who has no expertise about where they've been and they either won't talk at all or they'll tell horror stories to scare the person away. I really can't promise you a job, Trudee, and I don't want to give you false hopes, but what you've told me will make me view the kids and the issues from a completely different perspective. Give me a couple of weeks and I'll be in touch with you."

She didn't wait two weeks, but called me a week later. "I have a girl I'd like you to work with. I'm afraid there's no pay involved, but if we get you going we'll start looking for funding to pay you for full-time counseling."

The girl was only thirteen, an eighth-grader, Indian, from the inner city. She had been taken to Chicago by a pimp, worked there for a while, and then made it back home. Her mother had a problem with alcohol. The girl had refused to talk to the social services people at all.

I took a deep breath and dialed the number June had given me.

"Hello, is Julie there?"

"Who's this?" a child's voice asked suspiciously.

I explained who I was and said, "I know you've been involved in 'the life' for a while. I've been there too. I thought we could get together for lunch maybe and just rap about it."

It took a bit of persuasion on my part, of assurances that I wasn't a psychiatrist or social worker, that she wouldn't have to say anything, but she did finally agree to meet me.

It was hard to believe Julie was just turning fourteen. Her voice, mannerisms, and body were those of a tough twenty-year-old. I told her about my experience in prostitution: how I got in, how I got out, how much pain and self-destruction I'd been through. As I spoke, I felt her mistrust and contempt ease just a little.

"Julie," I said, "you can't grow as a human being or develop your own special beauty if you allow pimps to sell you and tricks to beat and pump away at your body."

Julie showed a cautious recognition and understanding of what I was saying. She didn't speak, but I could read her eyes: "How does this bitch know so much?"

We talked—or rather I did—for two hours in a downtown restaurant. Julie seemed almost relieved to hear someone mouth her exact fears and pain. The few questions she did address to me concerned how I got out—and stayed out—of "the life."

She canceled our next meeting, and I was afraid I'd lost before I'd barely begun. But I set up another one and this time she showed.

"I can't stand that motherfucking school!" she said intensely.

"Is it the same school you were in before you went to Chicago?"

"Yeah. Everybody in the whole school knows!"

Did I ever know how she felt! "Oh Julie, that must be terrible for you."

"Well, walkin' down the hall and havin' somebody call you a ho constantly ain't exactly a picnic."

"What do you do?"

"Kick ass, and then get suspended again."

I was amazed she went to school at all. "Has there been any discussion about an alternative school for you?"

"No."

"Would you like me to look into it for you?"

"I guess so, I sure can't take this any more. I got four years left at that school. I'll never make it!"

How could a girl like Julie, who'd been in Chicago giving blow jobs to men old enough to be her father and grandfather, relate to the Susies and Johnnys who were just beginning to hold hands?

"And I hate my mother," she spat. "She only uses me to clean house and go to the store for beer. The only time she likes me is when I drink with her!"

"Do you drink a lot?"

"Naw, I just usually get high on weekends."

Julie was starting to really talk to me. She herself brought up the subject of the tricks she'd been with.

"They really are disgusting! They ask you to do an

'around the world' on their dirty old ass. Man, I hated them tricks!"

"I don't blame you, honey. Did you feel like you had to do everything they asked?"

"Shit no, I wouldn't do anything weird or really filthy. I tol' them suckers they had the wrong chick. I'd rather see ten guys for twenty dollars and give 'em a straight fuck than do anything weird for three hundred."

I contained the fury I was feeling on her behalf. My anger wouldn't help her at this stage. "I just hate that you had to have these experiences, Julie," I said. "I'm so sorry that a nice person like you has had to go through this."

She looked surprised. I wondered if anybody had ever told her she was nice. It didn't seem likely.

"How old were you the first time you had sex, Julie?"

"Nine," she said matter-of-factly. "It was a neighbor boy, about fourteen. We were both drinking."

"Did you start drinking when you were nine, then?"

"No, earlier, maybe seven."

"This guy, the pimp, the one who took you to Chicago, what about him? Is he back in Minneapolis?"

"It doesn't matter, I don't want to talk about him."

Zap. I lost her just like that. The tentacles of fear seemed to reach out to grasp her brain. He'd really done a job on her, I thought.

"I'm not trying to get you to prosecute or anything. But I do want to make you feel good about Julie, 'cause I think she's a damn good little person!"

There it was again, that look, of surprise and bewilderment.

"I only want you to talk about the pimp to get rid of the feelings you might have about him, but we'll save that for another time."

When I left her this time, I patted her arm again and she didn't pull away, but seemed to lean in to it just a bit.

I called June. "She opened up a lot more today," I said, excited. "I can hardly believe it!"

"That's really good news. Do you think she's very vulnerable right now?"

"Hard to say. I know one thing: she'll never survive in that school."

June said she'd look into it. Then she asked me to speak at a conference for school social workers. "I'm supposed to do a thing on rape, sexual assault for them," she said, "but we could do it together. They'll even pay fifty dollars."

I was nervous as a cat the night of my debut speech. Jessie was visiting for the weekend and seemed very straight. We'd had a long talk about angel dust and I was hopeful that she might stop using it—and that she'd come home to stay.

When June came to pick me up, Jessie kissed me at the door. "Remember who you are, Ma," she said. "What you're doing is good."

Once I opened my mouth to speak, the words came pouring out. Suddenly I knew I had the audience in my grip. My feelings soared into rage and then softened, as I talked about the children on the Minneapolis streets.

Afterward, June told me over and over how good I was, and then she started booking me for all kinds of public-speaking engagements. I talked wherever I could to kids, parents, public-service people, and anyone else who would listen. Sometimes I got paid—thirty-five to fifty dollars from donations—sometimes I didn't. And though June gave me two more referrals, one from a family who could afford to pay me thirty dollars a session, I could barely support Joey and me. But the work felt wonderful. I was seeing Julie and about four other girls once a week—when they showed up.

Julie had finally decided I was safe and started talking about her pimp. "I'd been kinda messin' around with him, you know. I didn't know he was a pimp. Then he started this rap about makin' a lot of money and livin' good and headin' out for the Coast and livin' in the sunshine. By the time we left town, I think I knew he was a pimp," she admitted. "I just didn't want to face it. When we got to Chicago he said, 'This is it, baby, this is where you do your stuff!' I tried to refuse, but after a couple of black eyes I got in line."

"How did you feel about him?"

"I don't know. I guess it sounds pretty silly, but at first I thought I loved him, you know?"

"It's easy for a young girl to feel that, Julie."

"Well, he was real good to me, before we went to Chicago. I hated my ma and I wanted to get out so bad! I still hate her. I know she don't love me. You know what she told me today? She said I better make 'other plans'—I better find someone else to live with 'cause she's movin' away. How do you like that shit, man?"

"I know you must feel pretty bad."

"She calls me a ho all the time. I guess she's right about that."

"No, she isn't, Julie. You're a person, not a whore. You've had some bad experiences, but *you're* not bad," I said, taking her hand.

"I brought you something," I said, opening my bag. "Me? Why?"

"It's a Valentine present."

It was a simple card and decorator candle. Julie

started crying. I almost cried too. She got up and came around the table to give me a hug, embarrassed but determined.

Julie missed our next appointment and I had a feeling of doom as I put a dime in the pay phone to call her house.

"Oh, she's been gone for three days," her mother said nonchalantly.

"Mrs. Craig, have you notified anybody?" I asked.

"Well, the school called today. She probably went back to her pimp. That girl sure likes to get in trouble. I don't know what's wrong with her."

I got a cop from the juvenile division and we went looking for her. I hounded the pimp bars in Minneapolis and he followed lots of false leads. A week passed and still no Julie. I was terribly afraid the Chicago pimp had come for her. With the state of things at her house, she might even have gone willingly.

It was almost two weeks later that I dialed her mother's number again, hoping that she had heard from Julie.

"Hello," came a familiar voice.

"Julie! Julie! Is that you? My God, girl, where have you been?"

She was surprised that I was looking for her, that I cared enough to try and track her down.

"I stayed with this chick I know for a few weeks, just to get the hell away from my ma," she said. "I thought I was gonna stay there for good and get a job, a real job, you know. But we didn't get along too good."

"I wish you had let me know. I was really worried about you."

"Really?"

180

"Yes, really. Did you want me to worry?"

"No! I didn't even think about it. I just felt kinda bad about not showing for our appointment."

I didn't believe her. I didn't think she'd been staying with some chick. I was sure she'd been with a man, maybe a pimp. Julie didn't have many female friends. Once I had asked her if she had a best friend, and she'd said yeah—herself.

June and a couple of other people from social services tried to locate a suitable place for Julie to take refuge. There was none. So we formed a committee to lay the groundwork to establish a place. But that would take about two years at least. The best I could find Julie at the moment was the Adolescent Crisis Ward at a hospital, which I didn't feel was appropriate. Was it Julie who was sick? Or was it the society around her?

I hated meeting Julie to tell her I still didn't have a place for her.

That day, Julie's anger and pain came pouring out. "I hate my mother, I hate the kids at school, and I hate tricks and pimps!" Her tears fell on a roast beef sandwich and she abandoned it with a helpless gesture, burying her face in the white napkin. "I hate that bitch so bad! How could she treat me like she does? Could you treat your kids like that?" she cried. "She ruined my life! I'm so fucked up I don't know who I am! She just keeps tellin' me to leave, go back to the streets where I belong, I was always a ho! I can't take it, I can't take it. Where am I gonna go?"

I choked on my own feelings, and managed to say, carefully, "Julie, honey, I could get you into a crisis ward at the hospital."

"Hospital?"

181

"There's that or a foster home or a group home," I reminded her.

"I've been in a foster home, no thanks. And I guess I'm scared of the other girls in a group home. If they find out about me and stuff, you know?"

"Oh honey, I know you're scared, but we've got to try something. You can't go out on your own, Julie, you'll get eaten up out there again. You've got good stuff inside of you," I said, stroking her face, wiping the tears that she was unable to stop. "There's a beautiful, strong person inside there who needs a place where it's allowed to come out. Please believe me, Julie."

"Nobody else believes that! My mother doesn't!"

"That's because your mom doesn't believe in herself either. It's her problem, Julie, not yours. You have to let her work out her stuff. Let's us work out yours."

She agreed to go to the hospital the next day. I assured her it need be only a few days, but she was very depressed about it. I stayed there most of the afternoon and gave her a big hug when I left. She clung to me like a lonely baby, the street-girl toughness gone. I returned to see her the following day with posters to decorate her hospital walls. She told me she had attended group therapy; she hadn't said anything, but at least she had gone.

"A lot of people here have problems, with their parents and stuff," she told me.

I was very hopeful. Our time together was warm and loving.

"I hope you'll try to stick it out for a few weeks, Julie," I said. "We'll keep looking for a better place, but right now it's good for you to just get some rest and think about things."

When I went the next evening her mother was there. "I'm movin' to Toledo this weekend," she announced. "I brought the rest of your clothes, Julie."

That's it, baby. Cut-off city. Even if you get out, I won't be there or anywhere that you can find me. It was all I could do not to grab the woman and choke her.

I watched the two of them shake hands at the end of visiting hours. When I hugged Julie goodbye she clung to me again.

I couldn't reach her on the phone at any time the next day. I asked to have her paged, but still no response. Finally I reached the administrator.

"I'm sorry, Mrs. Peterson," she told me, "we think she may have walked out."

"What? She has no coat, no shoes, it's freezing out!" I said, my voice rising.

"We've looked everywhere for her. She did have a call earlier."

Again, I searched for her, and again I did not find her. Now her mother's phone was disconnected, so there was no one to even try to connect with. Several weeks went by and still she did not show up.

Goodbye, Julie, please remember that I think you're good and fine and beautiful. Don't let sick and lonely men bang your life out on dirty gray sheets in sleazy trick hotels, please child.

Jessie decided she wanted to go back to New York. I

was beginning to be ready too. I had heard of an organization there that was working with kids who had been or were in prostitution. I felt—and June stated it emphatically—that I had really helped in getting things off the ground in Minneapolis.

Back in New York, however, it turned out not to be so easy. The place I had planned to work turned me down for lack of experience or education or some other phony-sounding reason. I kept trying. I hounded the New York City child-care agencies, but nothing, nothing, nothing. I was almost hired by the Port Authority Police Runaway Division. I was one of the three finalists but I lost to a Master of Social Work.

Yet I wasn't sorry we'd come back, especially because Jessie and Joey liked their new high school—and we were together.

Finally, I met the New York City Runaway Squad and someone arranged an interview for me at a crisis-intervention center for runaways. I had tried and failed there once before. This time I was to see the head person. I opened the big glass doors to the administrative building. I had on my best beige pants and a brown sweater. I hoped I looked good, respectable. This was a feeling I still hadn't shaken—that I could never get respectable in a million years. It was as if I carried an old sign that said I was a whore, even though the sign was inside, where the scars were.

I gathered my courage and told the receptionist that I had an appointment with Mrs. Logan. "Take the elevator through that door and go to the fifth floor," she said.

I wanted to ask her what to do on the fifth floor but I thought it sounded dumb. As the elevator climbed, I thought about how important this job interview was. I

184

clutched my résumé and the letters of recommendation several Minneapolis professional people had given me.

The elevator door opened to another receptionist.

"Mrs. Able-Peterson?"

"Yes."

"Come with me."

I finally stood facing Mrs. Logan, who held out her hand and smiled a no-nonsense smile at me. Her stance told me she was a very busy woman.

I gave her my credentials and began selling myself. "Look, Mrs. Logan, I know I have no degree, no academics anyway, but I know these children. I've lived their life. I know the kind of self-destruction and pain they're living in. I really feel I could help you. I know from literature on the Center that you're working with a lot of child prostitution."

"Mrs. Peterson, I can think of a dozen ways in which the Center can use you. My only question is, how come you didn't come to us before?"

"I sent you my résumé."

"Hmm," she said, with a quizzical look on her face. "I'd like you to begin right away as a general counselor so you can learn about our organization, the way we work."

"If that's a job offer, I accept."

In these past three years, my life had changed completely. I was enormously involved with the kids I worked with, and somehow Joey and Jessie had flourished as well. They understood what I was doing, cared for my special ones, and, most important to me, they tolerated my concerns even when I brought my work home from the Center.

Before starting dinner this evening, I dialed Frank's number.

"Hi, Trudee."

Then the automatic first question: "Any news, Frank?"

"Nah, nothing. Unless someone comes forward with evidence, it's really gonna be hard unless—"

"Unless what, Frank?" I said. "Unless Heather's killer does it again, right?"

"I'm sorry, Trudee, under the circumstances it's very difficult to get any leads."

"I know. I guess I'm pretty tense. I have another kid in the hospital whose pimp did a number on her."

"Anybody I know?"

"Melissa Roberts. Just turned fourteen. Pimp's name is Artie. I think he's from the Bronx originally. About thirty."

"Doesn't sound familiar, but they could use other names on the street. She hurt bad?"

"Well, he stuck a bottle up her and cut her inside. She's got all kinds of infection from it. Bad enough?"

"Christ! She wanna talk to us?"

"Not at this point, she's too scared of him. The hospital is on alert to call you if he tries to see her. I don't think he knows where she is, though. They haven't seen him around the Center anyway."

"Okay, keep me posted, and if she changes her mind . . ."

I scrubbed some potatoes and put them in the oven. So Melissa can go home in a few days. Great. What would she do if I couldn't get a place for her in New York? She'd go back to the streets before she went back to Connecticut. I stopped and turned from the stove, the truth seeping into my thoughts. "She might go back to the streets anyway," I said aloud. I heard Heather screaming through a dark abyss of pain.

"What, Mom?" Joey asked.

"Oh sorry, honey, just thinking out loud." No! I won't let it happen to Melissa, Heather, I swear I won't.

The next morning I went down to see Melissa before going to work.

"Hi, baby. You look pretty chipper."

"I feel all right. When am I gonna get out of here? It's boring."

"Just relax," I said kissing her cheek, "not till Monday for sure."

"Damn, I don't feel sick!" she protested.

"You have no choice, little lady, so it will do you no good to pout."

She smiled sheepishly. "Can you come and see me this weekend?"

"Not Saturday, but I can make it on Sunday, okay? I think Friar Bill will come Saturday."

She grunted. I knew I'd hurt her. How many times had the door been slammed in her face?

"How's the girl in the hospital?" the receptionist asked me as I opened the Center door.

"Pretty good. She should be back on Monday. What's the in-house population today?"

"It was sixty-six this morning, about sixteen discharged and only four intakes so far."

"Thanks, I'm sure we'll make up for it tonight." By the next count there would be many more than sixty-six kids after evening intake. The Center walls were at the bursting point after fifty kids.

The pillows scattered around the small lounge were packed with young people from twelve to twenty. The radios blasted "Push Push in the Bush," and the young would-be hustlers leered at the more innocent and inexperienced runaways.

"Hiya, fellows," I yelled above the music. "Would you mind turning it down?" Ralph Valdez looked through my wool skirt, if that was possible, and reached lazily for the radio volume.

"Hi, Miz Peterson." He leered and snapped off the radio.

"Hi. Who's your friend?" I asked, gesturing at the handsome boy reclining beside him.

"My cousin."

"Hi, I'm Trudee Peterson," I said, sticking my hand out and smiling.

His eyes slid over me as he stuck his hand out without sitting up.

"Hi," he muttered.

I closed in on his eyes and tried to tell him I cared about him, nonsexually. Eventually, the boys stopped being sexual with me, but I had to prove myself each time. "Glad to meet you," I said. "Maybe the two of us can straighten your cousin out here."

The boys laughed; spontaneously, warmly, it sounded good.

188

* * *

I found Rick in the supervisor's office alone. He looked white and shaken.

"What is it, Rick?" I asked, closing the door.

"Trudee, Delia Liston was found dead in an abandoned building in the Bronx last night—overdose of Valiums." As he spoke, a single tear rolled from his eye to his chin.

Heather, Delia. Who would be next? I didn't want to go to sleep. I was afraid of my dreams. Now they would include Delia.

Why didn't you come to me and talk it out? Why did you face everything alone? Why didn't you let me help you?

I lit a cigarette and stared into the darkness. I remembered the hope in her eyes when she talked of going home to help her sister.

I put the cigarette out and turned over on my stomach, burying my face in my pillow. I didn't want Jessie to hear me crying and wake up.

I picked Melissa up at the hospital a few days later and took her to the Center. She was gone in a week. I notified both the Connecticut social worker and the

Runaway Squad. Did she go back to the pimp? I couldn't believe she'd do that, couldn't believe she wanted to hurt herself that much. Still, days went by and weeks and then months, and there was no word about her—or Heather's killer.

I kept calling Wayne at the Runaway Squad and Frank Barnes at Morals. Damn it, why didn't the kid at least stop by and tell me how she was? Was she ashamed, afraid? I thought we had begun to develop a relationship. Had I given her the wrong messages?

Then, as unceremoniously as she walked out, she walked in.

After I finished hugging her and hanging on to her very live little self, I asked her where she'd been, what she'd been doing these last couple of months.

It wasn't easy getting Melissa to reveal the details of her recent street life. But over the course of a few conversations, a composite picture of Melissa's day emerged.

Melissa reached for the phone over the litter of soda cans and gum wrappers on the bed table. She heard a glass thud to the thin green carpet below.

"Hello," she said sleepily.

"Check out time is one o'clock, miss," said the hotel clerk.

"Time's it now?" she asked, rubbing her eyes.

"Twelve-fifteen."

She hung the phone up and lay back on the bed. She dug in the ashtray and came up with a long roach, which she lit on her way to the bathroom.

The shower ran its cleansing feeling over her small body.

When she came out she opened her purse and counted her money. Two dollars and about seventy-odd cents' worth of change.

"Fuck." She threw the money back into the purse.

Dressed and on her way at 1:10, she dropped the key off at the desk and hit the streets—down Eighth Avenue toward 42nd Street.

"Yo, Melissa, what's up?" a voice called behind her.

"Hey, Chino," she said to the Spanish boy who came up alongside her.

"Where you headin'?"

"Get somethin' to eat, man. I'm starving," she told him.

"Got any money?"

"Not much, why? You broke?"

"Yeah. No luck with any fuckin' thing last night."

"Where'd you sleep?"

"Didn't, stayed on the trains."

"Well, I got enough to buy us a pizza and a soda, anyway," she offered.

They went into 42nd Street Pizza and ordered two slices of Sicilian and two Cokes. Some of Chino's gang, The 42nd Street Boys, sauntered in and sat down with them.

"Hey, Melissa, what's up?"

"Nothin'. I'm gonna try and get into the movies, you guys wanna come?"

"I got some smoke if you can get us in."

"I know the manager, he'll let us in."

Everybody was quiet for a minute. They all knew the score. Melissa would have to go to the manager's office and blow him. It was as accepted as the pizza they put into their young bodies for breakfast.

"Hey, *The Hot, the Cool and the Vicious* is playing a double with *Fists Like Lee*. Let's see that!" Melissa said excitedly.

"All right!" everybody said, slapping hands around the table.

191

It took her a few minutes to persuade the manager to let all of her friends in.

"C'mon, please?"

"All right, all right," he finally gave in. "See you upstairs in a few minutes?"

"I'll be there, don't worry."

They all found seats toward the front in the quiet theater.

"Be back in a few. Save me some shit," Melissa said, reminding them not to smoke it all while she was gone.

She climbed the side steps to the manager's cluttered office. He sat in his chair behind the desk.

"Come around here, baby," he said, motioning her around the desk. He already had his fly open. She knelt down between his legs, and her head just barely reached him. Afterward, she spat in the waste basket under his desk.

"Here," he said, handing her a tissue from the top of his desk.

"Could you give me a five?" she asked him. "I'm really tapped."

"Shit, I just let all your friends into the theater!"

"C'mon, Max," she wheedled, "please."

"All right, all right." He hated to say no to children, he always said; he had a *fondness* for them.

She bought five dollars' worth of sodas and candy bars from the counter downstairs and went in to rejoin her friends. They stayed through the two violent films and were back on the street at 6 P.M.

"I gotta go and make some money," Melissa announced. "See you guys later."

She was hungry. She wished she'd held on to some of that five for another pizza. She strolled over to Ninth Avenue and started uptown, walking very slow so she'd be visible. Now and then she stopped and loitered in front of a store. Finally she noticed a car that had circled her twice. The blue sedan pulled up beside her.

"You want something?" she said to the middle-aged man inside.

"You wanna go out?" he countered.

"Thirty-five," she told him.

"You kiddin'? I only want a blow."

"Thirty."

"Twenty."

"Twenty-five, baby, and that's it. I gotta eat too."

"Okay, get in."

He dropped her off at 42nd and Eighth and headed for the tunnel to New Jersey. He had to hurry, he had told Melissa, because his fourteen-year-old daughter had a part in the eighth-grade play and she would be terribly unhappy if her daddy was late.

Melissa went into the Flame Steak House and ordered their three-dollar special. It was a little tough but tasty. She poured ketchup all over her plate.

"Hey man, you seen Lexington Mary?" she asked the manager.

"Not today, hon. You want me to give her a message if I see her?"

"Yeah, tell her I'm headin' for GiGi's."

"Hey, Melissa, when you gonna come to my house?" he said, catching her arm when she paid the check.

"I'll be up one of these days and surprise you," she said, teasing him with her eyes.

The man had fed her a few times when she was tapped, and now he wanted his payment. She knew she wouldn't get any more free food unless she made it right with him, so she didn't go there any more unless she could pay for the food. You needed every friend you could get on the Deuce—she wanted to stay on his good side.

She walked up Broadway, calling to the other street kids she knew.

"Hey, you got any smoke?" she asked a young dealer.

"Sure, Melissa, how much you want?"

"Give me a nickel bag," she said, reaching in her jeans pocket for the money.

She bought a pack of Bambú papers at a candy store and kept walking up toward 45th Street. She decided she needed something for her head and approached the half a dozen or so guys outside GiGi's who were calling out, "Tuiys, acid, dust."

"What merchandise you got?" she said to a pock-faced boy of about nineteen.

"Tuiys, black beauties, and smoke."

"Give me four Tuiys," Melissa said.

She counted out the sixteen dollars for the four pills; she had only a dollar left from the twenty-five. She entered the disco atmosphere of GiGi's and went straight over to a drag queen at the bar.

"Hi, Mary, I was looking for you."

"Melissa, sweetheart, how are you, dahlin'?" the tall queen cooed.

"Wanna do some Tuiys with me?"

"Oh, child, I just did two about an hour ago, can't you tell?" Mary giggled.

"C'mon into the bathroom with me and we'll smoke." Melissa paid for a Coke with her last dollar and they headed for the bathroom. She handed the smoke to her friend to roll and popped two of the Tuinals into her mouth. The other two she tucked back into her jacket for later.

194

"So how's tricks, Baby-Street?" Lexington Mary asked her.

"I picked up a guy a little bit ago but I already spent the money. I gotta get somebody else soon if I want a room tonight."

"There were a couple of guys in here earlier lookin' for dates, but they wouldn't go with the queens—said they wanted real women. I told them suckers I was the most real woman they would ever find!"

They both laughed, sharing the street life they knew so well. Mary finished rolling the joint and they lit it up. When they came out of the bathroom, they hustled to a couple of songs. No tricks came in and Melissa decided she'd better go looking.

She didn't go far. Outside, a man began following her immediately and she stopped and looked into a store window to see if he'd approach her. He was really old—maybe sixty, she thought. Pretty soon she saw his image in the window beside her. She kept staring at the window.

"You wanna go out?" he asked.

"What you want?"

"Blow first, then regular."

"Fifty," she told him.

"Twenty-five."

"No way." Melissa began to move away.

It worked. "Forty," he offered.

"Where?"

"The hotel across the street."

They checked into one of the rooms on the lower floors, which were for rent by the hour. Melissa did what she had to and used the shower. When she came out the trick was gone already.

"Give me a double for the night," she told the clerk on her way out.

195

Maybe Mary would stay over with her tonight. It was better to share a room with someone. It wasn't so lonely, and it only cost an extra five. She counted out twenty-five dollars, collected the key, and took the elevator up to the room on the fourth floor. She rolled up the nickel bag and lay back on the bed to smoke a joint. The Tuinals had taken effect and she was beginning to feel nice. A few minutes' smoking later she went down again in the old elevator, which she now noticed smelled like urine.

Back at GiGi's, Melissa hung with Mary for a couple of hours, dancing and taking some more Tuinals. By eleven o'clock the disco was beginning to get crowded. She spotted her friend over by the door.

"Hey, Chino, you wanna stay with me tonight?"

"You got a place?"

She pulled out her key and dangled it in front of the boy.

"Damn, Melissa, I sure would appreciate that. I broke-night for the last two, and I'm ready to pass out."

"If you wanna crash, I'll take you over there now."

"I just took some speed, les' see if that works first."

"Okay, I'm goin' down to the Deuce and get something to eat, I'll be back in an hour."

She was more restless than hungry. She just walked around for an hour, bullshitting with other street kids, and ended up in the game room in the subway at Port Authority. Chino's partner was there and a girl she'd met a couple of times.

"Hey, Melissa, you seen Chino?"

"He was over at GiGi's," she responded.

"I was lookin' for him, man. I wanted to help him get

a place to crash, he been up for three days now, I'm worried about him, man."

"I told him he could stay with me tonight."

"Man, tha's really cool, Melissa, thanks a lot."

"You workin' too?" she asked the girl.

"Well, I was tryin' to, but this pimp won't leave me alone. He beat my ass twice last week. I ran away again yesterday. I'm really afraid I'm gonna run into him."

"Thas' fucked up. I know. I've had a lot of trouble with pimps too," Melissa said, remembering her own. "I try to stay away from the fuckers, but they be wantin' to get at you no matter what you do."

The girl nodded. "I been hidin' out down here and in the movies, but I'm broke now."

"Well, I'm gonna go back," Melissa said. "I'm supposed to meet Chino. Man, you want me to tell Chino anything?" she asked the boy.

"Jus' tell him I'll meet him tomorrow, same place as usual." The boy turned his attention back to the pinball machine.

Maybe I should have invited the chick to crash, Melissa thought. But I don't want no pimps bothering me.

She walked back across the Deuce, stopping to talk occasionally, and then back up to GiGi's.

"Give me two more Tuiys," she said to one of the dealers still gathered in front of the place.

"There's a lot of cars out tonight, Melissa," he said— a helpful reference to the car tricks that came out about midnight.

"Maybe I'll walk around a while. Thanks."

She pulled two car tricks and went back to GiGi's, through for the night. With forty-five on her, she bought two more Tuinals and looked for Chino inside. He was slumped over a table upstairs.

"C'mon," she said, shaking him awake, "you need some sleep." She half-carried him across the street to the hotel and propped him up in the elevator. She was feeling woozy herself from the six Tuinals, which didn't make her task much easier. Upstairs the two children fell on the bed and passed out. In the night she woke up to hear Chino crying and she struggled to get him under the covers and took him in her arms.

"Ssh," she rocked him, "ssh, it's okay, Chino. Ssh."

By this point in the story of her "day," Melissa was nodding heavily. Her head fell back.

"C'mon, babe, come with me," I said standing up and hauling her to her feet.

"Gotta sleep," she wailed piteously.

"Okay, c'mon," I said, half dragging, half carrying her dead weight to the elevator. I managed to get her into my tiny office. She slumped into the chair by my desk.

"What are you on, Melissa?"

"Mmmm?"

"Melissa, what are you on? C'mon, c'mon, talk to me," I said rubbing her hands and then patting her face.

"Inals," she slurred.

"Okay, Tuinals, what else? Melissa, what else?"

"Dust, acid!" she muttered angrily. Tuinals, angel

dust, and acid. What a combination. Most likely, it wouldn't hurt her, but she'd be out for quite a while. Just to make sure, I called for a volunteer nurse to check her over.

She was more surly with the nurse.

"Fuck you! Let me sleep. Fucking bitches always messin' wi' somebody."

"She'll be okay," the nurse assured me. "She needs to sleep it off. She can come to if she wants to. She probably hasn't had any sleep for a couple of days anyway."

"You're absolutely right. She likes to 'break-night' for a couple of days, and then crash for about thirty hours."

"Probably, if she has a nap, some of the effects will wear off. But she'll still be cranky when she wakes up."

"She's not exactly a bundle of joy now," I said, laughing. I was glad to see her alive, even in this condition. "She can sleep here. I'll do some paperwork and stay over till I think she's straight enough to go to the shelter downstairs. If she's still here in the morning when I come in, we'll start again."

It was six o'clock when she stirred. Actually, she moaned and stretched like a baby who has fallen asleep in a high-chair over a past-nap lunch. She looked like that baby too.

"Hi," I said, welcoming her back to reality.

"Ohh. Mmmm, shit, I feel terrible."

"I imagine you do from what you said you took."

"WhadIsay?"

"Tuinals, dust, and acid."

"Mmmmm."

"Well, is that accurate?"

"Whaddya mean?"

"Is that what you took?"

"I guess so. I took a lot, I know that. I took two ups in the morning too."

"When did you sleep last?"

She looked confused; she was still quite high, but not passing-out high. "Uh, I slept, uh, let me see . . . Monday night till Tuesday, I guess."

Today was Thursday. "What's it gonna be, Melissa? I can't handle another death. Look what you're doing to yourself! You look awful."

She was paper-thin, on pills and highs and irregular food, and no sleep and running all the time. She hung her head.

"Melissa, I want you to stay at the Center tonight and tomorrow we'll have a nice long lunch somewhere quiet where we can talk. It's time to take a good look at things, kiddo, and I'm here to help you do it, okay?"

"Okay," she said, taking a deep breath. "I'm starving!"

I felt she was straight enough for intake. The kids weren't allowed in the Center proper if they were high. Unless it was an overdose or something they really couldn't handle, like a bad trip. Then we usually sent them to the hospital.

I checked her in, sent her to dinner, and headed for the subway. She had promised me she'd be there in the morning. She'll probably sleep that long anyway, I thought.

I picked up pizza on the way home to give myself a break. When I got there, I found that Jessie had made one of her rare cooking appearances and had prepared pork chops. We ate both.

The next day Melissa agreed to give up "the life" and try the temporary group home.

200

"I'm so tired, Trudee. I don't think I can face the streets any more. I'm just tired. I gotta get away from the tricks before I do something really crazy."

She was ready. I had spent over a year talking to her, getting her to trust me enough.

"I want to leave the streets, but I don't want to. Is that crazy?" Melissa asked.

"I think I understand it, Melissa. I went through a period where I wanted desperately to leave prostitution, but I couldn't. I was afraid. What would I do? How could I start anything else? How do you fill out a job application? I mean, previous employment, prostitution! I also got used to the money. Although I never handled it well, I knew I had that earning power. I mean, it told me I was good at something."

"Yeah, that's it!" she said excitedly.

"But, honey, eventually I had to look in the mirror and see who I was in the scheme of things. It wasn't pretty just being a hole for the world to crawl in and out of."

"That's it too," she said. "I can't stand tricks, I hate them! I hate them so much. Sometimes I feel like murdering a trick, you know?"

"I sure do."

We were sitting on the window ledge in my office. Silently we stared down at the girls approaching customers on the street below.

"You know I'm really proud of you," I said after a while.

"Why?" she asked in a self-derisive tone.

"You seem to be talking much more openly about things. Here you are more able to face truths that are difficult for adults, and you're only fourteen."

"Almost fifteen!" she exclaimed, smiling.

I asked Melissa to stay. She seemed to want to be taken care of, and yet she was afraid of it, afraid to really put her trust back in the hands of an adult. I understood it and yet was entirely frustrated by it.

She said she now had a room she'd paid for almost two more weeks. She'd make a decision when the rent was up. I told her she was procrastinating and she agreed: she wanted desperately to be taken care of and it was beginning to show. She hung around the Center most of the day, left at night when I did, then reappeared the next day.

I gave her a few bucks to get some dinner. I wasn't supposed to, but I thought maybe it would keep her from turning a trick tonight.

On my day off I called in, but she hadn't been around. She knew my schedule. Most of my cases were like that: they would go to other staff for food or carfare or medical care, but when they wanted to talk they waited for me.

I didn't see her for a while again. I knew she was wrestling with leaving the streets, desperately wanting to and afraid to trust me at the same time. I knew I had no choice but to let her work it out. I waited—it was up to her now.

Finally, Melissa did stay, and she went from the Center to a temporary group home I had arranged for her. As a special-case counselor for sexually exploited kids, I was able to continue working with her and then to try to make funding arrangements for her to be placed permanently in New York City. I usually saw Melissa twice a week in my office, and once a week I took her out to do something special—lunch in a restaurant, a walk through Central Park—something normal to help her reintegrate herself into the society that had so neglected her.

Strolling through the Metropolitan Museum of Art one afternoon, she suddenly asked me, "Why do you think my mother gave me up?"

I had been expecting this for a long time. Not that I could answer it. "I don't know, honey. Maybe life was very hard for her."

She turned and sat on one of the marble benches. I knew her feet were killing her. I could see the flat white pumps pinching the sides of her feet. She had found them in the clothing donations, where she'd picked out the best things she could find with great care the day before, to dress for our special day. My heart turned looking at her little feet.

"Honey," I said sitting down beside her and leaning in to her, "how do you feel about your mother now?"

"I don't know. I'd like to find her."

"What would you say to her?"

She was silent as two Europeans strolled by looking at the Chinese vases displayed along the walls. She had said she liked Chinese art.

"I guess I'd ask her why she gave me up."

"Do you think you could ever be satisfied with her answer?"

"I don't know, but I'd like to ask," she said, her eyes filling with tears.

I reached for her hand. She was comfortable with my touch now. Her face screwed up, as if to shake off the emotions she was feeling. "Why do people have children they don't want?"

The oldest question, and the saddest.

*   *   *

Marty, too, became one of the success stories. He had started a new job in which he was doing well, and he had registered for night school.

"I sure feel better since I'm not hustling," he told me. "I met this guy too, we've been seeing each other for two months now," he said proudly. "It sure beats jumping from bed to bed."

Marty had come a long way. He was proud and rightly so. I was proud of him too. He still popped in to see me every few weeks.

One day he came in and announced that he'd been promoted from dishwasher to waiter.

"Well, if we're going to celebrate your promotion, we should do it right, don't you think?" I said. We went to lunch at an outdoor café.

The waiter took our order and left us. A slight warm breeze was blowing around us. I leaned back in my chair and stretched, the sun felt good. Martin laughed.

"What's funny?"

"You look like my mother's cat stretching in the sun."

"Have you heard from your mother lately?"

"I called her last week."

"And?"

"It was okay. It's just that she pretends that everything is hunky-dory, like nothing had ever happened. Like I was away at college or something."

"To be fair, Martin, she doesn't really know what you've gone through."

"What does she think kids go through when they leave home at fifteen?"

"Some people see only what they want to, honey."

The boy tugged unconsciously at his sweater sleeves, pulling them down to hide his frayed cuffs. I made a mental note to look for some decent shirts his size in the donations. I wanted to take him down to Macy's and buy him some. Unfortunately, it wasn't in my budget.

"Well, I wish she was strong enough to face the truth. I get tired of carrying it around by myself."

"I know you must, Marty," I said, looking into his beautiful sad eyes. But today was supposed to be a happy day. I tried a new tack. "Are you excited about your new job?"

"Kind of," he said guardedly. "I guess I'm scared too. I mean, what if someone recognizes me? What if some trick walks into the restaurant and tells them who I really am?"

I looked hard at him. "Who are you really?"

"I don't know." Martin lowered his gaze.

There had been one half-hearted suicide attempt in the past year, but recently he'd seemed quite stable. Loneliness was Marty's problem—yeah, and that of two million other people in this city, I thought. The instability of bed-hopping really got to him. This was a common problem for gays, whose relationships were often very brief. For a person like Marty, who was capable of and needed some depth, it was downright destructive. I hoped his "new friend" would work out. My two oldest friends had been together for eighteen years and I always told them they had outdone all the so-called straights I knew.

*   *   *

I considered Martin and Melissa, so far, pretty successful cases. God knows there were few! But at least I knew that if I hadn't been there, they could more easily have ended up like Heather and Delia.

Iris had continued to be unreachable. At one stage I had been able to learn something about her background. She had been introduced to sex at age seven by her mother's boyfriend. Her mother found out when it was discovered that the child contracted gonorrhea. The mother threw the man out, but he moved into an apartment just a few buildings away. She was afraid of him, afraid to turn him in. He threatened to kill her, and Iris too. Her mother tried to protect Iris, even went outside with her when the child wanted to play. Then, when Iris was eleven, her mother died.

Iris went to live with her aunt on the next block. She was ashamed to tell her aunt anything about her experiences and decided to keep it a secret. But it started again. He would catch her coming out of school, in the playground. Sometimes he even waited in the hallway of her aunt's building. When Iris couldn't take it any more she ran away.

Within two days a pimp had her, and she was on the street. At age twelve, Iris was working, fourteen, fifteen, sixteen hours, day and night, getting into car after car, never knowing if she would get out.

During the last of our rare sessions at the Center, she talked a lot about how she felt about her customers.

"Boy, would I ever like to off one of those mothers! Those people don' deserve to live."

She said it many, many times. Just as Melissa did, and the others—including me.

"Iris, honey, get away from them. It would be easier to get away from them than to kill them. Why should you spend the rest of your life in jail?"

"At least I'd have someplace to be then, somebody to take care of me."

Here it was again. That nobody-wants-me feeling. And I couldn't blame these kids: it did look that way.

Still, I had to try. "Somebody will take care of you, Iris. You can go to your aunt's house, she sounded very concerned about you."

"They don' really wan' me! She tells you that shit. You don' know what it's like there. There's not even enough food for her kids!"

"Okay, then, a group home." All I could think of—alas.

"I been there. I don' like it," she said, shaking her head adamantly.

"Isn't it better than tricks and the Delancey Street Strip?"

"I don' know! I din' like it! They didn't treat me right there either."

"Oh baby, they're never gonna treat you right on Delancey Street, never, ever."

Iris did, in fact, leave Delancey Street: her pimp moved her uptown to the Times Square area. He probably believed business was better there, or perhaps she was hot on Delancey Street—and, besides, he could observe her more closely to be sure she didn't come in to the Center for counseling on how she could get away from him.

207

Every day I saw her from my office window. Every day I watched Iris take trick after trick around that corner. It was beginning to drive me crazy. I couldn't talk to her, couldn't approach her, because I knew her pimp would beat her for talking to me. I couldn't find out anything about how she was. All I knew was that Iris's little body went around that corner ten, twelve times on my shift. I tried to stay away from the window, yet I was drawn to it like a magnet.

"She still out there?" Jimmy Kelly asked, coming up behind me.

I jumped like a thief. "Oh, Jimmy, it's like she's saying, 'Look at me, look how bad I am. You tried to help me and look how bad I am.' I can't stand watching her and I can't stop either. Do you think she's shooting?"

He shrugged. "I don't know, Trudee. Whenever I see her up close she looks pretty high. But it could be downs."

I wept, overwhelmed by my helplessness.

I felt it was time to get out there again and observe the kids in action on the streets. Maybe I could think of a new approach, a new way to get them to come in for help. At least I'd see who was still out there. And I was especially worried about Beth, who had been at the Center a few times. The last time she had stayed for a while and I had begun to hope or to think maybe—I was making some progress with her. I thought she was tired of getting beaten by her pimp, Lucky. She did go home to her family upstate; then one day she just disappeared again.

I told Frank my little history with Beth. He knew Lucky. "It gets depressing," he agreed.

Frank was so good for me to talk to. I drew

tremendous strength from knowing that a man—a cop, no less!—could understand what these kids were going through and that he felt what I did about the sexual abuse of these young people. I didn't get to see him or talk to him as often as I would have liked because we both had our work to do. I had even trained myself—now that a year had gone by—not to ask him about Heather's killer every two minutes. I had never given up thinking about it myself, but I figured it was time to leave Frank alone about it.

We were driving slowly down Eleventh Avenue. Garbage and other debris littered the gutter along both sides of the street. Behind it and against the backdrop of abandoned, gutted buildings, the young girls milled about, walking up and down, their walk suggesting that they were for sale. They wore flashy blue and red and black Spandex pants and high-heeled boots.

"See anybody you know?" Frank asked me.

"No, but that's not surprising, if they haven't been to the Center I wouldn't know them."

One girl standing alone on the corner appeared to be about thirteen. "She looks like a young one," Frank said, voicing my thoughts. She stared into the car, anticipating a customer. I tried to smile at her but decided she might take it wrong: many of the girls had couples as clients. Her eyes, haughty and defiant, shot me a look of hatred: Don't stare at me, you bitch. Who the fuck do you think you are? She swung around and started walking toward the Hudson River.

An abandoned building behind some of the girls seemed to be staring at me with its big black holes that once were windows. I knew some of the kids slept in those buildings when they were running from their pimps. I couldn't imagine walking in, much less sleeping there with the rats.

I watched out the window of Frank's car as we turned east on 23rd Street. Neon signs advertised pizza, souvlaki, deli. These were the lights of the playground for the children of the evening. The drizzle that started when we were up at 39th Street stopped as abruptly as it had begun. The girls wouldn't get a break tonight; some of the pimps were easier on them when it rained hard.

When we were as far east as Second Avenue, Frank headed downtown again. "Do you want to see the Delancey Street Strip?" he asked me.

"You're the driver."

It was a busy night. I hoped I wouldn't see any of my girls. The route seemed to be to walk a block off Delancey, then back, then off. Deals were made on the off street.

An older model Oldsmobile pulled up to the sidewalk, and a girl of about sixteen with very high heels and a rabbit coat went over. She leaned in to have a word with the driver and then got into his car. They drove off to some desolate spot to take care of business. I hoped he wouldn't hurt her—and inevitably, I thought of Heather.

"The girls don't make big money down here," I said.

"No," Frank agreed. "It's mostly fifteen- and twenty-dollar blow jobs—ten even."

As we drove slowly by, the girls glared at us. They didn't much like sightseers. One girl gave us the finger. I didn't blame her. Living in her misery was enough, she didn't need people staring at her as if she were part of a sideshow. For free, too. Several of the girls looked high. I knew this to be an area where there was a lot of drug taking, and most of the girls were hooked on something.

A cute little Puerto Rican girl sauntered in front of our car. She looked like Iris and my heart jumped a minute till I was sure it wasn't Iris.

I wondered if there were mothers and fathers somewhere who had lost their daughters and could have found them here. None of the girls looked very old. We drove around and around, staring at the same sordid scene. Finally, Frank pulled up in front of a club on Allen Street near Delancey and stopped the car. We could see several guys playing pool inside.

"This is where a lot of the pimps wait," Frank told me.

I looked in at the flashily dressed men luxuriating by the pool table, drinks in hand, waiting for the flesh of their girls to translate into cash for them.

"Let's go," I said. "It makes me nervous when they look at me. I've always hated pimps."

We headed uptown again. We went through the garbage-strewn streets of the East Side. I hadn't yet seen any girls I knew, I was thinking, when I realized that Frank was saying something to me. I finally registered what it was.

"What do you mean, they found Heather's killer?" I nearly screamed.

"You didn't know?"

The girl's face loomed before me. "Frank, who?" I said, my voice breaking.

He pulled over to the curb and shut off the engine. He turned to look at me. "I'm sorry, Trudee, I thought you knew."

I guess I had stopped nagging him one time too soon. I couldn't bear to hear it, and yet I knew I had to know everything. I reached into my pocket and dug out a shredded tissue. I blew my nose and swallowed.

"Why did he cut her legs off?" I asked in a small voice.

"I think I'd better tell you the whole story. There was a witness, another girl in the room when it happened."

I listened in silence, visualizing the scene.

It was a quiet night for Heather and her partner, Lettie. They sat in a small diner on the West Side in the 30s.

The guy kept begging them to go with him. "C'mon, girls, give me a shot. We'll have a good time."

"Get outa here, you ain't got any money to spend," Lettie said.

"Not a whole lot, but I got some coke and we can get a bottle and have a good time. I could give you each forty."

Heather's ears perked up. She was always ready to get high. It was the only thing that took away the pain. Sometimes she said she wanted to drown in booze.

"Look, if we don't pick anything up soon, well, maybe," Lettie said, shrugging her shoulders.

"Okay, look," the man said, standing up, "there's a little bar on Twenty-eighth and Eighth. I'll be there, meet me there."

He turned and walked out of the diner. The girls stared after him for a moment. Heather saw him get in his car and drive away.

"You ever been with him?" she asked the other girl.

"Nah, but he hangs around all the time. All the girls know him. You know how some guys hang around hos all the time."

"Well, we sure ain't had shit yet, man, and I wanna get high. Think he really got some coke?"

"Yeah, he uses it. I've helped him score before."

"Fuck, what's the use, why not?"

The glaring fluorescent lights of the diner were not kind to Heather's old-young face. Puffy from all the alcohol consumption, she looked closer to thirty than to seventeen. Her beautiful red hair was losing its natural sheen and looked dull. Her hand shook as she picked up the coffee cup.

"Anything else, girls?" the old blond waitress asked them.

"Nah, give us the check," Lettie said.

"The guy paid," the waitress informed them.

Heather and Lettie smirked at each other. As they stood up, Heather doubled over for a minute.

"You okay?" Lettie asked.

"Yeah, I get these pains," Heather explained. She hoped it wasn't another dose. That would put her out of commission for too long.

"Listen, let's walk over and go down Ninth—maybe we'll pick up something on the way," Lettie suggested.

"You don't want to go with this guy?" Heather asked.

She did, she knew she could get high and obliterate the night if they did. She'd even have a few bucks for the rundown pimp she was with. Maybe he wouldn't beat her. She didn't care much if he did, she was used to that. It even felt right sometimes, made the other pains, the ones inside, go away.

"I don't give a shit really," the other girl said as they walked along the dirty street. "I guess he's all right."

Heather didn't know Lettie very well. They were working together because their pimps were friendly. She shivered in her light coat. It seemed she was never warm enough. She meant to buy a warmer coat, but most of the money she made just paid the hotel bill and bought the drugs for her and the pimp. She didn't make very good money any more.

"Here's one," Lettie said as a black car pulled up.

"You girls workin'?"

"That's right, fella, what you want?" Lettie asked.

"A blow job. Just one of you, though."

"How much and which one?" Heather said impatiently.

"Ten, you," he said, looking at her.

"Fuck off." Heather walked away.

"Fucking whores, that's all you're worth!" he yelled, pulling away.

"You shoulda tried to talk him up," Lettie complained.

Heather clamped her mouth tight and refused to say anything else. They picked up their pace heading toward the bar on 28th.

It was dark and dirty inside and smelled of old beer and whiskey. Lettie recognized one of her customers and went over to talk to him. Heather walked up to the man they'd been talking to in the diner. He was sitting at the bar and she climbed on the stool beside him. The bar where she leaned her arm was sticky and wet; she didn't care.

"We on?" he asked.

"Sure. Get me a drink, will ya?"

"Give the lady a drink," he said to the bartender.

She drank a double brandy, in one gulp, setting her glass down for more like a thirsty child.

By the time the three of them left the bar, they were pretty high. They snorted some coke in the car and drank out of a bottle he kept in the glove compartment.

"Where goin'?" Lettie slurred.

"Don't worry. I got us all hooked up," he said confidently.

Heather thought they went through the Lincoln Tunnel, but she didn't know New York very well. She rarely got out of midtown. Riding in the car felt good. She wasn't cold any more. Lettie pulled out a joint and they shared it as they drove through the night.

"I hope we ain't goin' too far, man," Lettie warned him.

"We're almost there," he said, digging his nails into Heather's leg. He pulled into a motel parking lot on the side away from the office.

"Be right back," he said, opening his door.

"Hey, leave the blow," Heather begged.

He handed her the little bottle and the coke spoon and walked to the office. Heather and Lettie took two big snorts apiece and put the cover on. Heather picked up the whiskey bottle and took a slug, wiping her mouth with her hand. She coughed spasmodically for a minute, spittle dripping down her chin. She doubled over for a minute.

"Bitch, you sure can drink a lot," Lettie observed.

The man was back beside the car in a few moments. "Let's go," he said, his mouth tensing.

The shadows from the motel lights made them all appear furtive, as they were. They walked to the back entrance, up a flight of concrete stairs, through a door to the second-floor hallway, and down the green-stained carpet to Room 27.

Heather flopped on the near bed and took the bottle out of her purse. She took another swallow and handed it to the man.

"Where's the coke?" he demanded.

"Right here. Don't get fuckin' excited," she said, reaching into her pocket.

The man had a blow and took off his jacket. Lettie took her clothes off and piled them on the table. The man finished undressing, and he and Lettie tumbled on the bed beside Heather. She could hardly feel them beside her. Her brain was numb. She struggled up finally and went for the bottle on the desk.

"Ow, you son-of-a-bitch, don't bite so fuckin' hard!" Lettie yelled.

"Take your clothes off and join us," the man told Heather. She set the bottle down on the table and methodically removed her clothes. When she got to her shoes, she stumbled and fell, hitting the chair. She lay there for a minute until she heard him call again, "C'mon bitch, get with it." She got up on all fours and, reaching for the bottle again, crawled to the bed, spilling the whiskey on her arm. She set the bottle on the bedside table, after taking another drink, and climbed up on the bed. Her body rolled to their weight and she felt all the arms and legs. She started giggling.

"What's so goddamn funny?" Lettie asked.

"Centipede, we're a fuckin' centipede," Heather said, still giggling.

At first the man didn't touch her at all and she just bounced along with the motions of the other two.

"I told you not to bite me, motherfucker," Lettie yelled again.

Heather focused on them in the 69 position beside her and reached for the bottle again.

"Let's have another blow so you two can loosen up," the man said, getting up. He brought the coke to the bed and held the spoon for each of them. Heather was floating in space. She felt good, warm kind of.

216

"Now it's your turn," he said, grabbing Heather's breasts.

He arranged the girl in the missionary position, entered her, and started pumping. Heather felt nothing. The pain in her side didn't even hurt. She didn't feel Lettie get off the bed and go sit in the chair by the window, smoking another joint and watching the couple on the bed. Heather was hardly moving or making any sound. She just lay there passively as the man kept pumping. Lettie finished the joint, and they were still engaged. She was glad she hadn't gotten stuck with this part of it—this fucker could go on forever.

"Goddamn it," the man said.

Heather only wanted to reach for the bottle again. She imagined how the whiskey would taste going down her throat.

"Dirty motherfucker," the man swore again.

Lettie watched him flip Heather's body over. "Get up, get up on your hands and knees," he commanded.

Heather heard him from far away. She wobbled and struggled to her hands and knees. She felt him plunge into her from behind and winced a bit. She reached for the bottle, which was now close to her, and managed to take a swig as she rested on one elbow. She dropped the empty bottle on the carpet.

Lettie again appreciated that she wasn't in Heather's position. She thought she'd gotten the better end of the deal. She slumped in the chair sleepily.

The steel blade in his hand seemed to appear out of nowhere. Lettie had not seen a knife before. The blade flashed for a moment from the street light outside. Lettie watched in horror as the man grabbed Heather's red hair, pulled her head back and slit her throat, in one movement.

Heather never screamed, but Lettie thought she heard a gurgling noise. Afterward, she wasn't sure if it had been the trick having an orgasm or the blood in Heather's throat. The trick moaned and slumped over the dead girl.

A scream began in Lettie's throat and her hand flew to her mouth as her body bolted upright. The trick jumped up and made a frightened sound, backing away. He stared at the knife for a few seconds, then laid it carefully on the desk behind him. He stared transfixed at the body on the bed and reached for his genitals, holding them as if to protect them. He realized Lettie was in the room and turned to her. She backed toward the window.

"Don't be afraid," he said nervously, "don't be afraid, I won't hurt you. Oh my God, what have I done. Oh my God!"

Lettie stood frozen by the window, afraid to speak or move.

"We've got to get her out of here! You've got to help me, we're in this together!"

"Please don't hurt me," she whimpered, "please."

"Let me think, let me think," he said, putting his hands to his face. He saw the blood on them and pulled them away in horror. He went into the bathroom and began washing.

Lettie took the few steps to the desk and grabbed her clothes. She went back to the window and started pulling them on, staring at Heather's lifeless form. She thought she saw a dark stain on the bed.

When the man came out he turned the light on. That was when Lettie began to scream.

"Shut up!" he yelled. "Shut up!" He took a few steps toward her.

She froze again.

Heather lay still in a huge pool of blood. Her arm dangled down and almost touched the empty bottle on the floor.

The man grabbed the side of the bedspread and began rolling Heather in it. He tried to lift the body but couldn't. He tried again.

"Go into the bathroom and clean yourself up," he ordered Lettie. "Go on!" he yelled when she didn't move. "Don't come out till I tell you to!"

Lettie could hear him grunting as if he were exerting himself very strenuously. She sat on the toilet seat, staring at the wall. He called to her. She didn't move. He banged on the door. She didn't answer. He tried the door and it opened. He slapped her.

"No!" she screamed, putting her hands up in defense.

"Look, you gotta help me, bitch. C'mon." He grabbed her arm and pulled her into the other room.

She saw the two objects wrapped in blankets and sheets; she refused to let herself think about what they were.

"I'll take the big one down to the car and you carry the smaller one," he said.

Lettie nodded.

The man looked out the door before they entered the hallway. Lettie's bundle was heavy, but she was able to handle the weight—besides she was too scared not to. She felt the warmth of its contents and shivered. They carried their bundles to the car and put them in the trunk.

"Look, you'll be implicated in this, so you better

keep your mouth shut," he warned her as they pulled away from the motel.

"I won't tell, I won't, I promise."

He drove for about fifteen minutes and stopped the car in a desolate parking lot.

"What are you doing?" Lettie cried.

"Just sit there and shut up," he ordered.

He went to the back of the car and opened the trunk. She heard a thud. He must have dropped the body, she thought numbly.

They drove forward and she never saw what lay behind them: the half body of a girl with red hair, a girl who was never loved, only used—the final use, his ejaculation for her life.

I was crying all through the story Frank was telling me.

"Trudee," Frank said kindly, "I'm so sorry."

"Why didn't he kill the other girl?" was all I could say.

"That kind of a killer, the sexual kind, only has the impulse to kill for orgasm. Once the orgasm is over, he's spent. He has no desire to kill: in fact, he probably can't."

"What did he do with her legs?"

"I don't know, Trudee."

"Oh Heather," I said to her sweet image before me. I saw her gentle, sad, passive eyes, the pretty blueness of them. That tiny weak smile she gave me those few times. I remembered telling her her red hair was like my mother's.

I pulled on the door handle and leaned out, gagging.

I knew there were cases where men who did such things—murdering prostitutes, to be precise—were acquitted when they were brought to trial. Sometimes there was insufficient evidence and other times the testimony against them was discounted because it came from "questionable" witnesses. It was entirely possible that the person who killed Heather, the man the police were holding right now, might be free again in a year or so—free to repeat the whole ugly scene. I wondered who would be next.

I kept thinking of Melissa. She couldn't stay much longer at the temporary group home. She wasn't really happy there, anyway, I soon found out. When I came back from a brief vacation I learned that she had tried to take her life. She'd gone on a weekend spree of angel dust, and when she returned to the group home she was found in the bathroom with a razor. I was so relieved that she'd been stopped in time. I couldn't lose her now—we'd fought too hard and come too far.

I talked about it with her and she admitted that she'd been afraid and angry when I wasn't there.

I took her to see a psychiatrist, who prescribed an ongoing relationship with her social worker, me. It scared me: it felt like too much responsibility. What if she hurt herself? Would I be to blame? I wasn't sure if I knew where to draw the line. I knew it had largely been my influence that got her off the streets. I believed I could keep her off because I believed that, inside, it was what she wanted too.

I would do everything I could, everything I knew how to do for her. I prayed that would be enough.

"Well, baby, are you ready?" I said to Melissa when I picked her up to help her transfer to a permanent home I had arranged for her.

"I'm kinda scared."

"I know. It's another change, and that's hard. But I'll

221

still be here. That's not gonna change." I hoped I sounded reassuring.

"Okay," she said softly.

We had barely arrived at Melissa's new group home when an attractive young woman greeted us. "Hello, I'm Justine, your new social worker," she said.

Melissa's eyes darted to me. "I've got a social worker—Trudee is my social worker!" she protested.

"Oh, I'm sorry. I meant I'm the social worker for the house. You'll still be seeing Trudee, but you can see me too."

"Honey, it's okay," I said as soothingly as I could. "She just means that she'll be here too if there are any problems in the house for you."

"I don't need another social worker," she muttered.

A black girl walked into the room. "Hi, Melissa, remember me? I was in the other group home with you last month."

"Hi," Melissa said, warming up a little.

"Come on, I'll show you around," the girl offered.

The girls left the room. "It's just that she needs time," I said into the stares of the social worker and house mother. "We've gotten very close and she has begun to trust me. She's really come a long way, really."

They both looked doubtful.

"Well, she'll have to spend some time with Justine," the house mother explained rather coolly.

"Look," I said, "this girl has been on the run for four, five years. She spent the last nearly two years in Times Square. She's dealt with abandonment, adoption, foster homes, physical and sexual abuse by *family*, prostitution, drugs, gangs, peep shows, you name it. She really hasn't had much reason to trust adults. It's taken me a long time to get her to trust me and come back to this world. She's a very dear little person when you get to know her, but she does take some patience and understanding. She's worth it."

"I'm sure they all are," the house mother said, "but they have to be able to fit into the house, follow the rules, and cooperate."

"Why don't we give her some time and a little space," Justine suggested. I could have kissed her.

"Thanks," I said to Justine when the house mother left. "I really don't want to blow this one. I've been working on her for a long time. She's really had a shit life, you know?"

"It sure sounds like it. I read the file when it came over yesterday. You've really put some work into this girl. Seems like it's starting to take. I'm amazed you got her into group care at all."

I felt warm inside. "I love her."

"I can see you do, and she obviously responds very well to you. Listen, I'm not going to go pushing in with Melissa. I can see that would be harmful for her. If we just take some time maybe she'll relax. I agree with you—I don't think she should lose the stability she's gained with you."

"I really appreciate that, Justine. Maybe if we schedule a meeting together with her and let her feel she has some power over the situation. She feels threatened right now, new house and all, new girls."

"That's a good idea," Justine said, just as the house mother returned. "I think Trudee and I have figured out an approach to working with Melissa," Justine told her.

She raised her eyebrows; it was impossible to read what she was thinking.

Melissa came back into the room. "It's nice here," she said to me. "My room is really nice too. You wanna see it?"

"I sure do," I said, standing up. We climbed the two flights of stairs. "It is nice, Melissa. You can do a lot with this room. We can get you some posters and things for the wall, and you can decorate it and really make it your own."

"You'll still be my social worker." It was a statement rather than a question.

"You're not getting rid of me that fast," I assured her, putting my arm around her. "I'm pretty hard to shake."

She smiled shyly. "I'll stay if you're still my social worker."

"Honey, I just had a talk with Justine. She really seems like a decent sort. Since she knows the house and the girls and staff better than we do, I think we should try to work with her."

She looked scared.

"Look, I'm only saying that we—*we*, Melissa—will work with her. I'm not saying she'll replace me, okay?"

We talked a bit about the new home and the adjustments she would have to make, and the fact that I would be there when she needed me. Melissa seemed relaxed and in a good mood when we parted. She and the other girls already had plans to go roller skating on the weekend. Please make this work for her, I prayed as the cab took me back to Times Square.

Just a few days later, I had a call from the house mother. "Have you heard from Melissa?" she asked me.

"Not since yesterday. Why?" I said, tensing.

"She AWOLed last night. Left the house about eight,

224

saying she'd be back for ten o'clock curfew. We haven't seen her since."

"Damn. Well, I haven't heard anything. Was she with anybody?"

"A young man picked her up on a bike."

"I didn't even know she was seeing anyone right now."

She simply said, "Call if you hear from her, please."

"You won't discharge her will you?" I asked.

"Not right away. It depends on how long she stays gone. Did she do this very often in the other house?"

"No, an occasional time or two," I lied. Melissa had always had a problem with curfew and AWOLs. The staff at her last house had been exceptional with her, giving her enough time to adhere to the house instead of ejecting her after the first two AWOLs. Eventually she had learned that they cared for her and that was why they wanted her off the streets early, not that they were punishing her. It was hard for kids who were used to all the freedom they wanted to start coming in at 10 P.M. At the other house she had even learned to deal with being on restriction when she did break the rules. But it had taken almost the whole four months for her to adjust. I didn't know if this house and its house mother would be willing or able to go that far with Melissa. To be fair, the other house had been more transient, with kids coming and going. Melissa had been one of their longest residents because I was working out the funding. This new house was more stable, with permanent girls, they couldn't let Melissa do what the other girls couldn't get away with. "If she comes in, will you call me, please?" I asked before the house mother hung up. "She needs this placement, whether she realizes it yet or not. I'm sure she'll adjust soon."

Minutes later, my phone rang again. It was the Center's receptionist. "Trudee, Melissa Roberts is here to see you. She's really a mess."

She hung her head when she walked into my office.

"You better hang your head! Where have you been?"

"The bike broke down in Long Island. We didn't get it fixed till this morning. We almost froze!"

"Melissa, how can you get on a bike and go to Long Island at eight when you know your curfew is ten?"

"He had to go to do something."

"Number one, who is *he?* Number two, why did you have to go with him?"

"He asked me to."

"Oh, that's a good piece of logic, great. If I asked you to throw yourself in front of a speeding locomotive, would you do it?"

"No," she said, sulking.

"Who is this guy?"

"A friend."

"Is this *friend* worth blowing the group home for?"

"If they don't want me there, I'll leave," she said defiantly.

"I didn't say that. But you knew before you went there that there would be rules, right?"

No answer.

She continued staring at the floor. I didn't say anything as I sat there, waiting for her to come to terms with her guilt and anger.

"Am I discharged?" she finally asked.

"Do you want to be?"

"No," she said, a bit arrogantly.

"Well, you're not." I thought I saw relief on her angry little face. "I think the house mother is worried about you. She called me this morning, just a few minutes ago in fact."

Melissa grunted, making a face.

A few days later she came home high on Tuinals and was put on more restriction. The house was beginning to get tense about her. Justine seemed to understand and she helped me to keep the peace. And to keep Melissa in. She needed time to act out and not be thrown away for it. It was the problem in a lot of families: kids began acting out and their parents told them to hit the road. We all felt it at certain stages: sometimes I noticed it in my own kids. It was important to hang in there with them. Most of them outgrew this acting-out behavior when they began to mature. It was hard on parents, but once kids were out of the house, they could be damaged so much by the streets that it could only go from bad to worse.

What happened next in the Melissa saga was an unexpected blow for both of us. My supervisor decided that I couldn't spend so much time with her. I was to wean her so she wouldn't be so dependent on me.

"Look, when she's ready to let me go, she will. This is nonsense!" I said hotly.

"You're overinvolved, you need to get farther away from the case. You're just not able to be objective about her, Trudee," my supervisor said.

"You're damn right I'm overinvolved, and look at the progress she's made. This is her first relationship in years, her first trust maybe ever! You can't just take that away from her now—I don't care what the books say!"

I was able to see her one time each week instead of three: Melissa had to go to her house mother or the other social worker, she had to learn to develop relationships with other people. I remembered an incident a few weeks before. I was bringing Melissa back to my office when we ran into the head of the volunteers.

"Oh, Trudee," she said, "I wanted to talk to you about doing another training session for the new volunteers."

"I've been kind of busy," I told her, "but give me a list of times and I'll let you know."

"I'd really appreciate it," she said, turning to smile at Melissa. "Are you a friend of Trudee's?" she asked.

"No, I'm her baby!" Melissa said confidently.

When I now explained the new routine to her, she asked distrustfully, "How come I can only come once a week?"

"Well, honey, there are others who would like to get to know you too. The house mother is awfully fond of you. I think they would like you to feel like you can count on them too!"

"I guess you don't want to see me so much? Is it because I've been in so much trouble at school?"

"Melissa, it's not anything you've done. Nobody has done anything. It would be good for you to get to know some of the other staff a little better. Justine is very nice, don't you think?"

"Guess so. I can't talk to her, though."

"Have you tried?"

"I don't want to talk to anybody else. They don't understand!"

"Melissa, look, that's what life is, dealing with all different kinds of people. Getting to know and communicate with and getting along with different people." I was trying to persuade her of something I did not even approve of.

I tried to be unavailable as much as possible. I felt like

228

Judas. It hurt me to put her off. I tried to be firm, but my heart wasn't in it.

Finally, she left the group home.

I asked all the other kids to keep an eye out for her. I knew she'd show up in Times Square somewhere. Where else would she go?

Four days, five days, no word. I clung to the hope that she wasn't working the streets or peep shows. A week passed: it was the longest period in six months that I had gone without seeing or talking to her. Maybe she wouldn't come to me this time. Maybe she felt rejected and wouldn't reach for me.

At last, it was Marty Elkins who brought me news. "I saw Melissa last night."

"How is she? Where is she?"

"I saw her at a disco in Times Square. I told her you were probably worried about her and she should get her little ass over here!"

"Where's she staying?"

"With some dude. Sounds like he's straight, not a pimp. I'll probably see her again tonight. She said she wouldn't come back to the Center, not ever again."

"Marty, ask her to call me tomorrow morning, please. Tell her we can have breakfast together."

The next morning the phone rang ten minutes after I got to the office. "Hello, Trudee speaking."

"Hi."

"Where are you?"

"Just down the block."

"Want some breakfast?"

"Yeah, I'm starving. I didn't eat yesterday."

"Meet me at the diner on the corner. I'll be there in five minutes."

I grabbed her and gave her a big hug. "Where have

229

you been? You've had me worried to death, girl!"

She accepted my affection like a lonely puppy. "I can't take group homes anymore. I just want to be free. It doesn't feel natural there. Everybody's always poking into your shit. I don't want to live there. I won't."

"What are your alternatives?"

She shrugged.

"Where are you staying?"

"With this guy."

"What guy?"

"He's okay," she said defensively. "He's got a job, he works."

"How long have you known him?"

"For a while."

"We're getting nowhere fast. How do you feel about this guy?"

"I like him a lot. There's just one small problem."

"And what is that," I asked, handing her a menu.

The waiter came over to us. "Ladies, what'll it be?"

"What do you want, Melissa?"

"Eggs and toast and bacon. I'm starving!"

"How do you want your eggs?"

"Not hard and not soft, so I can dip the toast."

"Just coffee, please. Milk?" I asked her.

"Chocolate milk."

"What's the one small problem?" I asked when the waiter left.

"Well, he used to go with this girl. He doesn't go with her anymore, but . . . well, she wrote to him and she might be pregnant."

"What then?"

"Well, he says he doesn't love her any more."

"But what if she's pregnant?"

"I don't know."

"Oh, Melissa, how can this work out? It doesn't seem as if your friend is really free."

"He's supposed to talk to her tonight. Then we'll know."

She seemed shaky. Obviously she thought she might lose out on this deal.

"Melissa, I'm going to give you my home number. If things get bad for you, I want you to call me. And come home." I said the last quietly and surely. I had made up my mind.

Her eyes widened in surprise. "Really?"

"Really. I've been thinking about it for a long time. I've talked to my family about it, they've agreed." It was true.

Neither one of us said anything. I guess it had to sink in for both of us. I knew I would lose my job if the Center found out. Or at least be in danger of losing it. Two of the hard and fast rules were No kids in your home and Don't give out your home number. I hadn't ever broken them till this minute.

It happened faster than I thought it would. The whole day was way out of the ordinary. That afternoon I had a call from the school social worker of my daughter's friend Terri who wanted to place Terri at the Center. Terri had lived with us before, she had left home many times and ended up at our house. But we hadn't seen her much in the last two years. Still, I couldn't let her be referred to the Center, it was like having your niece referred for shelter. I called Jessie at home.

"We can't let Terri go to the shelter, Ma. She's not used to street kids."

"I know," I said. I was so proud of Jessie. I told her I'd also offered Melissa a home.

"Is she coming?"

"I don't know, honey, I guess we'll just have to wait and see."

"Where we gonna put everybody?" Jessie asked.

"I don't know. I guess we'll have to stack them up," I said. We both laughed.

My home phone rang at 2:30 A.M.

"Hello?"

"Trudee," Melissa cried in a small voice, "remember what we talked about this morning? Well, she's pregnant and she's there. I came home after giving them some time to talk and he met me at the door. She's staying."

"You sound pretty high, babe. You okay?"

"Took some Tuiys and other stuff. I'm okay, I guess."

"Can you take down some instructions, or remember them?"

"I think so."

Forty minutes later I stood out in the cold night, wondering if I could handle what I'd taken on. The taxi pulled up; I paid the driver and helped Melissa into the house.

Jessie got up and asked her if she wanted anything.

"I'm so thirsty."

"Want some Perrier?"

"Okay."

Melissa took one sip and said, "Yuk." I don't think she knew what Perrier was.

"I'll make up the couch for her, Mom," Jessie offered.

"Good idea. We'll talk about things in the morning. Try to get some sleep, honey, and maybe tomorrow when you're not high we can talk things out."

"I don't know if I can sleep."

"Try, honey. Welcome home," I said, tucking her in and kissing her good night.

I must be crazy, I thought, lying there in the dark. But at least Melissa wasn't on the streets. We'd have to make do with whatever we had. She needed a home, Terri needed a home. I needed to give them that.

All day at work I kept expecting a call telling me I was fired. It had been hard for me to go against the Center rules. But I just felt Melissa's best shot was with me. There was absolutely no one in her life except me.

At midday I walked through Times Square and watched the kids from the Center "in action." I saw one boy selling joints on the corner and another one weaving around, probably on Tuinals. Several girls I recognized were working in front of the porno theater pulling lunch-hour tricks.

I left work a little early that afternoon. Terri was at the house too and all three girls were watching a soap opera. Melissa still looked sleepy and kind of vague.

"Aha, stimulating," I announced. "What's happening to poor Laura Baldwin?"

"She was raped by Luke Spencer, but it wasn't rape really, and she won't tell anybody who did it," Jessie offered.

"You like soaps too?" I asked Melissa.

"Yeah, we used to watch them in the group home," she said shyly.

"Jessie feed you?"

"Uh huh."

"I made eggs and toast for her, Ma. And I took a chicken out for dinner."

Later on I took Melissa into the back room to talk to her privately.

"How do you feel?"

"All right."

"It must seem strange to be in my home."

She nodded.

"Well, honey," I said, taking her hand, "as you can see, we don't live too fancy. There's really not enough room for us all, but I'll put some extra effort into looking for more space. In the meantime, you're more than welcome to share what we do have. It ain't much, but it's yours, babe. Okay?"

"Uh huh."

"Honey, it'll be strange for a while, but give yourself time to get used to it. If you need to talk about anything, let me know. I want you to understand that this decision to take you is very important to me. If I lose my job, which I doubt, but if I do, that's okay. I mean it, Melissa, if I do, we'll make out okay. This was my decision and I'll take the responsibility. So I want you to know right now that if anything like that happens, you're *not* responsible. Just let me worry about that stuff."

"I was thinking about that. I feel better now."

"Okay," I said, giving her a little squeeze.

Times Square was a hard habit to break, it was all she knew, where she felt accepted. The weekend came, and that's where she went. I had given her weekend spending money along with the other kids. Although I talked with her about it a lot, I didn't forbid it. I felt she had to work it out of her system. To forbid it might make her split. If she could be pulled into the mainstream of our family life, she'd give up Times Square, I knew it.

I wasn't fired, but two months later I was awarded a fellowship I had applied for in the Charles M. Revson

234

Future of the City program. I started school at Columbia in a few months and received fifteen thousand dollars plus full tuition. I was overjoyed, I needed to get away from the Center. I was feeling frustrated. Oh yes, there were the girls who had left prostitution, but they always had somewhere to go, an aunt or grandmother, some family member who had been willing to step in. They had a place to be while we worked things out—consciousness, image, feelings. But the girls who didn't have that kind of long-term shelter and support were still out there. I wanted very much to be able to start an experimental house, a long-term residence. But it wasn't easy. First of all, it couldn't get zoned. But, in addition, certain experts thought the girls shouldn't be separated from the other kids. I didn't—and don't—believe we can get anywhere with these kids unless we can keep them long-term. I could use the fellowship year for learning and contacts. Saying goodbye to the kids was next to impossible. I told them I'd still be working for them, but in a different way. I told them I wasn't leaving them. It all sounded hollow and empty as they sat across from my desk one after another. I felt like a deserter no matter what I said to justify it. But part of me knew it was right; I had to do more for the kids. I would have to try to build my own organization for these children. I prayed they'd stay alive until I could really help them.

The text of this book is set in 11 point Palatino.